CANADIAN CONCEPTS

Second Edition

3

Lynda Berish
Sandra Thibaudeau
Collège Marie-Victorin

Prentice Hall Allyn and Bacon Canada
Don Mills, Ontario

Canadian Cataloguing in Publication Data

Berish, Lynda, date
  Canadian concepts 3

2nd ed.
ISBN 0-13-591702-6

1. English language—Textbooks for second language learners.*
2. English Language—Grammar. 3. English language—Grammar—
Problems, exercises, etc. I. Thibaudeau, Sandra, date. II. Title.

PE1128.B473 1996   428.2'4   C96-931530-9

Allyn and Bacon, Inc., Needham Heights, Massachusetts
Prentice-Hall, Inc., Upper Saddle River, New Jersey
Prentice-Hall International (UK) Limited, London
Prentice-Hall of Australia, Pty., Ltd., Sydney
Prentice-Hall Hispanoamericana, S. A., Mexico
Prentice-Hall of India Private Limited, New Delhi
Prentice-Hall of Japan, Inc., Tokyo
Prentice-Hall of Southeast Asia (PTE) Ltd., Singapore
Simon & Schuster Asia Private Limited, Singapore
Editora Prentice-Hall do Brasil Ltda., Rio de Janeiro

ISBN 0-13-591702-6

Acquisitions editor: Dominique Roberge
Developmental editor: Marta Tomins
Production editor: Elynor Kagan
Editorial assistant: Rita Self
Production coordinator: Sharon Houston
Design: Monica Kompter
Layout: Joseph Chin
Text illustrations: Heather Collins
Unit opening illlustrations: Carole Giguère
Cover image: Walter Schmid/Tony Stone Images
        "Front Street with Gooderham Building, Toronto."

Printed and bound in Canada

6789 IG 098

To Millicent and Max Goldman for their support in many ways over the years.

CONTENTS

To the Teacher
Page ix

LISTENING ACTIVITIES	GAMES AND ACTIVITIES
1. Nice To Meet You	Find Out A Frequency Survey
2. I'm Calling About an Apartment	The Apartment Building Puzzle Find Someone Like You
3. I'm Looking for a Job 4. A Job Interview	What's the Job? Job Ratings Job Tic-Tac-Toe
5. I'm Your New Neighbour 6. I Was Wondering... What's the Weather Like?	Spot the Differences Categories
7. An Invitation to Dinner 8. I Was Wondering... What Time Do You Eat?	Food Ratings Quick Review

The World

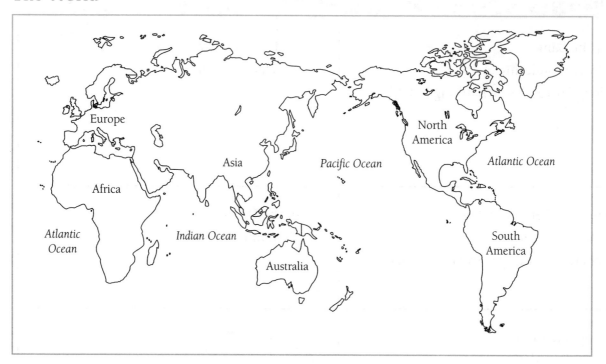

Canada

TO THE TEACHER

The *Canadian Concepts* Series

The new edition of the popular *Canadian Concepts* series retains the Canadian focus designed to help students feel at home and integrate into the community. In the new edition, exercises and activities have been graded and, in some cases, refocussed to provide a careful build-up of skills throughout the series. *Canadian Concepts 1* is paced to accommodate the needs of post-literacy students, while *Canadian Concepts 2* moves ahead to introduce new vocabulary and grammatical structures at a faster pace. *Canadian Concepts 3* provides a richer field of vocabulary and a greater degree of challenge while reinforcing the themes of the lower levels. *Canadian Concepts 4, 5,* and *6* integrate video materials on Canadian themes.

The *Canadian Concepts* series uses a communicative approach. The method offers productive strategies for language learning based on student-centred interaction. Many new activities, games, and opportunities for speaking have been incorporated into the series to encourage maximum student participation in classroom activities. The pedagogical model presents students with challenging listening or reading input, leading them through pre-activities and strategies that make the input comprehensible. In addition to these fluency-building activities, dictation, grammar, spelling, and vocabulary work focus on improving students' accuracy.

Canadian Concepts 3

Canadian Concepts 3 builds and expands on themes from *Canadian Concepts 1* and *2*. It provides ample practice in all skill areas. Listening, speaking, reading, writing, grammar, pronunciation, and vocabulary-development exercises are integrated into units in interesting and relevant ways.

Canadian Concepts 3 is made up of ten self-contained thematic units. Core activities focus on dialogues and reading texts. They are designed to provide students with the language they need for their daily lives. Follow-up activities recycle language and concepts and lead the students into meaningful practice contexts.

Each unit begins with a short quiz to introduce new vocabulary. Many new listening activities have been added, including "I Was Wondering" dialogues, which answer questions about life in Canada.

Each unit concludes with Ten-Minute Games and Activities to review and extend new vocabulary and structures.

Students gain confidence to function in English from the practical topics and cultural information presented in the book. They are motivated to use their new skills in the real world through the Community Contact Tasks. Throughout the book, language is carefully graded to help students become more proficient and more confident as they move through the text.

Teachers and students will appreciate the simple format and lively appearance of the materials, with clear illustrations that lend valuable visual support. They will also enjoy browsing through Canadian Capsules that provide background information on Canada. The audio cassette tape has been recorded with concern for natural Canadian speech patterns. Worksheets to accompany many of the activities in *Canadian Concepts 3* are provided in the Teacher's Manual, with permission to photocopy.

KEY TO SYMBOLS

    Listening activity

Reading activity

Writing activity

Work with a partner

   Work in a group

Journal activity

Role-play activity

Teacher's Manual

A comprehensive Teacher's Manual provides step-by-step instructions keyed to the student book, answer keys, tape scripts, and teaching notes. Teaching tips and suggestions for optional activities for use in multi-level classrooms are incorporated.

Detailed teacher's notes are included to clarify the intention of activities and to make suggestions for promoting interaction in the classroom. These ideas will be appreciated by new teachers, while experienced teachers will find that the materials lend themselves to flexible interpretation and accommodate individual teaching styles.

At the End of the Course

Students who successfully complete this level will be ready for *Canadian Concepts 4*, which features practical and interesting themes with a wide variety of activities and discussion topics. Video activities are introduced, with CBC programs providing lively topics for listening and discussion.

UNIT **1**

GETTING TOGETHER

Class 1

QUIZ: NAMES AND GREETINGS

Before you start the unit, try this vocabulary quiz. Work with a partner. Choose the best answers.

1. North Americans usually have at least:

   a) one name

   b) two names

   c) four names

2. Another word for "family name" is:

   a) pen name

   b) surname

   c) given name

3. A nickname is:

   a) a formal name

   b) an informal name

   c) your parent's name

4. Initials are:

   a) the letters of your first name

   b) the letters of your last name

   c) the first letter of each name

5. A polite greeting is:

   a) "Nice to meet you."

   b) "What's your name?"

   c) "Why are you here?"

6. "What do you do?" means:

   a) "How are you?"

   b) "What are you doing?"

   c) "What is your job?"

1

WHAT'S YOUR NAME?

 Work with a partner. Ask and answer these questions.

1. What is your first name?

2. What is your last name or surname?

3. Do you have a middle name? What is it?

4. What does your name mean?

5. Do you have the same name as someone in your family? (Are you **named after** someone in your family?)

6. Do women change their family names when they get married in your culture?

7. Do you have a nickname? What is it?

8. What are three popular girls' names in your culture?

9. What are three popular boys' names?

10. What are three common family names in your culture?

FAMILY NAMES

A Work in groups. Make a list of ten North American family names that you know (e.g., names of neighbours, famous people, or teachers).

B Read the story quickly.

Family Names

People who come from North America usually get their last names or surnames from their families. The last name, or surname, is the same name that the parents have. It is called the family name. Parents generally give a first name, or names, to their children.

Long ago, people had only one name. A man could simply be called John or Peter. A woman could be called Mary or Elizabeth. After some time, there were too many people with the same names, so second names were needed. A child took the father's name as a last name. In this way, the children of John, for example, were called Peter and Mary Johnson. Names such as Wilson (Will's son), Jackson, Anderson, and Davidson came into use.

Many Scottish and Irish names are common in North America. "Mac" or "Mc" means "son of," so the name MacGregor means "son of Gregory," and MacDonald means "son of Donald." "Fitz" is another way of saying "son of." It comes from fils, which means "son" in French. Fitzpatrick and Fitzgerald mean "son, or child, of Patrick and Gerald."

Not all people got their second names from their fathers. Some got their names from where they lived. For example, a family that lived in a village with many green trees could be called Green or Greenberg. If a family lived near a field, it could take the family name Fields.

Sometimes people got their names from the way they looked. A tall person was, perhaps, called Long. If people in a family had dark hair, the family was sometimes called the Blacks or the Browns. If their hair was light, they may have been called the Whites.

People often took their names from the kind of work they did, too. A person who sewed clothing was named Taylor. Another person who baked bread was called Baker. A person who had a very good voice was named Singer.

After a while these names stayed with people and became family names that are still used today.

CANADIAN CAPSULES

Men in Canada sometimes use nicknames to greet each other. "Joe" is the most popular nickname, but "Mac," "Jack," and "Bud" are also used. The expression "an average Joe" is sometimes used to represent an ordinary person, the "man-in-the street."

C   Work with a partner to answer the questions **orally**.

1. How do people in North America usually get their surnames today?

2. How do they get their first names today?

3. How many names did people have long ago?

4. Why did people need more than one name?

5. How did people get their new names, at first?

6. Give two examples of ways to write "son of."

7. Copy the chart below. Show three ways people got their names. Give examples of each.

Ways to get name	Examples

D   Work alone. Write answers to the questions in your notebook.

 GRAMMAR FOCUS   **Present Simple Tense**

Use the present simple tense to describe things that don't change or actions that are habitual.

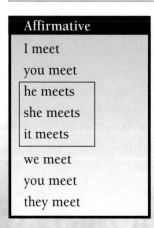

> The sun rises every day.
>
> I wake up at seven o'clock.

Form the simple present tense with the base form of the verb. Add **s** or **es** to the base form with **he**, **she**, and **it**.

> The sun (it) rise**s**.
>
> I wake up at seven o'clock.

Affirmative
I meet
you meet
he meets
she meets
it meets
we meet
you meet
they meet

Words and expression such as **always**, **usually**, **sometimes**, **generally**, and **every day** can be used with the simple present to show the frequency of an action or habit.

A Complete the sentences with the correct form of the verb.

1. My friends _____ for coffee **every morning.** (meet)

2. People **usually** _____ hands when they meet. (shake)

3. The teacher _____ new students to the class. (introduce)

4. Aki's friend _____ tea to coffee with his meals. (prefer)

5. The weather _____ quickly in Montreal. (change)

6. Parents **generally** _____ names they like for their children. (choose)

7. Marco _____ English by chatting with his friends. (practise)

8. The sun _____ hot in the spring and summer. (feel)

9. A child _____ a family name in North America. (need)

10. The neighbours _____ their fish **every day**. (feed)

11. A family _____ an important role in most cultures. (play)

12. Parents **often** _____ about their children's friends. (worry)

13. We **sometimes** _____ the bus to go to work or school. (take)

14. A newcomer **usually** _____ to be introduced to people. (want)

15. Kim _____ a lot of new friends at school. (have)

B Choose the verb. Put it in the correct form.

**stay help speak enjoy introduce be take come want
arrive work**

Olga is a student in our class. She studies English after work twice a week. She is very friendly. She usually __1_____ new students to other people in the class. She often __2_____ the teacher hand out papers.

Sometimes Olga __3_____ late at her office to finish her work. Then she __4_____ late for class. She is so nice that nobody __5_____ angry when she is late. She __6_____ her seat quietly and __7_____ with her partner.

Olga and her partner __8_____ different languages. Olga __9_____ from Russia. Her partner is Vietnamese. They __10_____ to learn English. They both __11_____ the class very much.

FOCUS ON EXPRESSIONS

A   Match the expression with their meanings.

1. Nice to meet you.

2. What do you do?

3. I'm fine.

4. kids

5. Nice to run into you.

a) children

b) I'm pleased to meet you.

c) I'm OK.

d) It's nice to see you again.

e) What is your job?

B   Read the sentences in each pair. Are they the same or different? Write **S** (same) or **D** (different)

1. a) It's nice to run into you.

   b) I'm pleased to meet you.

2. a) I'd like you to meet my kids.

   b) I'd like to introduce my aunt.

3. a) I'm fine, thank you.

   b) I'm OK, thank you.

4. a) It's nice to meet you.

   b) I'm pleased to meet you.

5. a) What do you do?

   b) What are you doing now?

6. a) I'm happy to see you again.

   b) It's nice to run into you.

7. a) What does she do?

   b) What's her job?

CANADIAN CAPSULES

McIntosh apples are famous all over the world. These apples are named after an Ontario farmer. In 1880, John McIntosh planted an apple orchard in Upper Canada (Ontario). Most of the apples were bitter, but one tree had delicious apples. McIntosh grew more of this kind of tree. Today, every McIntosh apple can be traced back to this original tree.

NICE TO MEET YOU

 A Read the questions aloud with your partner.

 B Listen and answer **T** (true) or **F** (false).

1. Amir and Nadia are married.
2. Maria works in a bank.
3. Maria doesn't like her work.
4. Amir works in a small store.
5. Nadia is a nurse.
6. Nadia works full time.
7. Nadia and Amir have three children.
8. Nadia and Amir have two girls.

C Write correct information for the sentences that were wrong. Use your notebook.

Turn to page 11 for Exercise D.

ROLE PLAY: INTRODUCTIONS

A Work with a partner. Write a conversation to introduce two of your friends who don't know each other. Use phrases such as:

Have you met…

This is my friend…

I'd like to introduce…

B Act out your conversation.

SMALL TALK

A Choose the questions people usually ask in North America when they first meet.

1. How old are you, Mrs. Brown?
2. Did you watch the hockey game Saturday?
3. What do you do, Ted?

4.   How many children do you have?

5.   How much money do you make?

6.   Why aren't you married yet?

7.   Where does your wife work?

8.   What is your religion?

9.   Did you go away on holiday this year?

10.   How much did you pay for your dress?

11.   When are you going to have children?

12.   What are you doing?

B   Which subjects do people usually not talk about when they first meet?

C   Do you know some conversation topics that are acceptable in some cultures and not acceptable in other cultures?

CHATTING

A   Work in pairs. Use the words listed to complete each paragraph.

movies
interest
topics
person
time

When people in North America meet for the first __1_____, they talk about subjects of general __2_____. They talk about the weather, __3_____ or entertainment, school, work, or local events. These are topics that you can talk about if you don't know the other __4_____ well. They are good __5_____ to use when you want to start a conversation.

children
polite
married
subjects
people

__6_____ in North America do not talk about things that are personal when they first meet. Some __7_____ are private and it is not __8_____ to ask people about them. For example, people talk about their families, but they don't talk about why they aren't __9_____ or why they don't have __10_____.

jobs
health
weather
religion

It is not polite to ask a person's age or weight. People ask each other about their __11_____, but it isn't polite to go into details about how they feel. People often talk about their __12_____, but they don't talk about their salaries. Topics to avoid are politics, sex, and __13_____. Safe topics include the __14_____, sports, and holidays.

questions
nosey
public
friendly

When two people meet in __15_____ they don't ask __16_____ about why the other person is there or what the other person is doing. These questions are not seen as __17_____. They are probably seen as __18_____.

B   Work with a partner. Use the information in the paragraphs to answer the questions **orally**. Do not write your answers.

1. Name four subjects of general interest.

2. When are these good topics to use?

3. What are two questions about families that are not polite?

4. What are two other questions that are not polite?

5. When people talk about their jobs, what should they not talk about?

6. What are some general topics to avoid?

7. Name some safe topics.

8. What are two questions people don't ask another person when they meet in public?

C   Work alone. Write answers to the questions in your notebook.

JOURNAL: ABOUT ME

Write a paragraph to introduce yourself to your teacher. Write about yourself, your family, your interests, and your reason for studying English.

TEN-MINUTE GAMES AND ACTIVITIES

Find Out

Walk around the classroom and talk to different students. Complete the chart with information from different students. Write the information in one column, and the source (the name of the person who gave you the information) in the second column.

	Information	Source
a date of birth	August 2nd, 1974	Mario

1. a date of birth

2. the name of someone's brother or sister

3. a food someone ate for breakfast this morning

4. a sport someone plays

5. someone's favourite song

6. the name of a movie someone liked

7. the kind of pet someone has

8.   the name of a book someone read

9.   a kind of food someone likes

10.   a city someone has visited

11.   a kind of music someone likes

12.   a colour someone likes

Share your information with the class.

A Frequency Survey

Work in a group. Ask each person in the group these questions to complete your chart. Use the worksheet.

100%	always
	very often
	often
	sometimes
	rarely
0%	never

	Student A	Student B	Student C
How often do you:			
1. watch a sunrise?			
2. sleep in until noon?			
3. meet a friend for lunch?			
4. walk more than a kilometre at a time?			
5. spend time with your sister or brother?			
6. read a newspaper from another city?			
7. eat popcorn at a movie?			
8. cook dinner for a friend?			
9. play a sport outdoors?			
10. clean your cupboards?			
11. read a story to a child?			
12. make a long-distance phone call?			
13. send a fax?			
14. play computer games?			
15. buy a birthday gift for someone?			

Share interesting information with the class.

NICE TO MEET YOU

LISTENING ACTIVITY 1

  D Listen and complete the dialogue. Use the worksheet.

Maria: Hi Nadia. How _____ you?

Nadia: Fine, thanks. Nice to see _____ again, Maria. Have you
met my husband, Amir?

Maria: No, I haven't. _____ to meet you, Amir.

Amir: Nice to meet you too, Maria. Nadia has told me a _____
about you. Do you still work in a bank?

Maria: Yes, I work in a bank downtown. _____ a teller.

Amir: Do you like it?

Maria: _____ all right. The work is interesting. How about you?
What do you do?

Amir: I work in a large store. I sell computers _____ office
equipment.

Maria: Are you still working at the hospital, Nadia?

Nadia: Yes, but only part-time. It's hard to be a _____-time nurse
when you have small children.

Maria: How old are your kids now?

Amir: Our daughter is four, and _____ son is seven.

Maria: Oh, they're still pretty small. I guess you two are really busy.

Nadia: We are. Well, nice to _____ into you.

Maria: Yeah. Nice to see you too. Nice to meet you, Amir.

  E Work in a group of three. Practise the dialogue.

UNIT 2 MOVING IN

Before you start the unit, try this vocabulary quiz. Work with a partner. Choose the best answers.

1. This takes you up in a building.

    a) a railing

    b) an elevator

    c) a slide

2. If you live in an apartment, this is a place to grow plants.

    a) a yard

    b) a cupboard

    c) a balcony

3. This person looks after an apartment building.

    a) a police officer

    b) a caretaker

    c) a supervisor

4. In an apartment building, the washing machines are in:

    a) the garage

    b) the lobby

    c) the laundry room

5. If you live in an apartment, you should not make noise after:

    a) 10 o'clock

    b) midnight

    c) 11 o'clock

6. If there is a fire you should not use:

    a) the stairs

    b) the elevator

    c) the fire escape

Where do you live? Work in a group to discuss these questions.

1. Do you live in a house or an apartment?

2. How many rooms do you have?

3. How big is your building?

4. How many floors are in your building?

5. Does your building have an elevator?

THE APARTMENT BUILDING

A   Look at the pictures of people in different parts of their apartment building on page 15. You can use some pictures more than once. Find:

1. a balcony   6. the basement

2. an elevator   7. the garage

3. the laundry room   8. the front door

4. the mailboxes   9. the roof

5. the lobby

B   Use the words below to complete the paragraph.

**elevator   balcony   hall   apartment   lobby   bedroom
kitchen   floors   basement**

Margaret lives in a large __1_____ building. There are fourteen __2_____ in the building. There is a staircase for emergencies, but most people take the __3_____ up to their apartments.

Margaret's apartment is on the ninth floor. She lives alone, so she has a small apartment. Her apartment has a living-room, a __4_____, a small bedroom, and a bathroom. She likes her apartment because it is very sunny. She has a small __5_____ off the living room, where she can sit outside when the weather is nice.

Her friend Patricia lives down the __6_____ . She lives in a two-__7_____ apartment with her husband and their baby. Margaret often meets Patricia in the __8_____, where they go to do their laundry. Sometimes they meet at the mailboxes in the __9_____ when they go downstairs to get their mail.

IN THE APARTMENT BUILDING

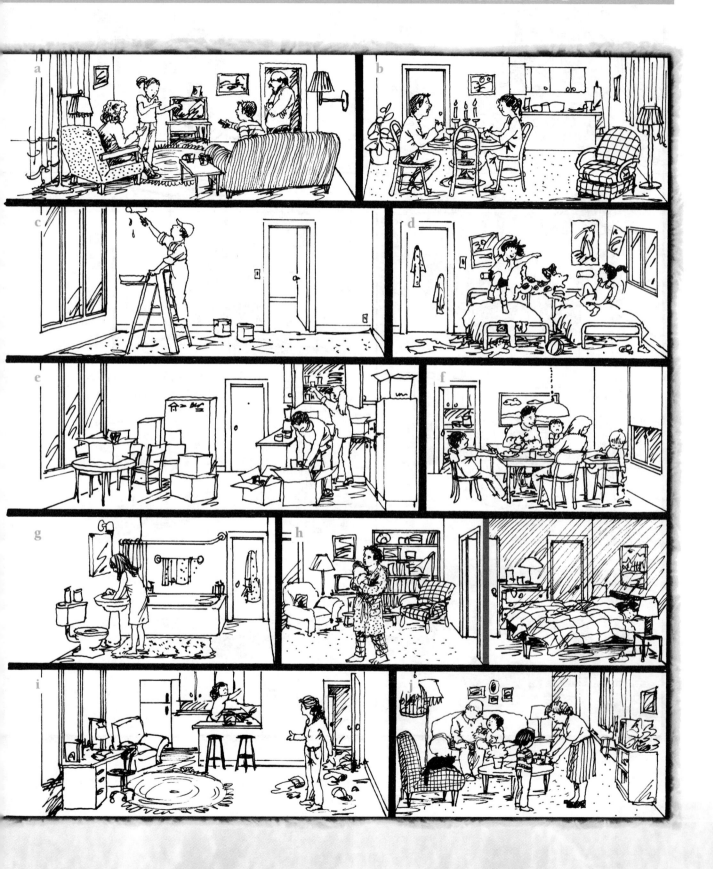

A   Read about the people in the building. Then match the description to the apartment.

In the Apartment Building

1. In this apartment, a mother, a father, and three young children are eating dinner. The children are not happy because they don't like the vegetables that the parents cooked. Their parents like vegetables. Their favourite is broccoli. The children only want to eat french fries.

2. The couple in this apartment just got married. They like to cook together, but they have a problem: the man is vegetarian but the woman loves to eat meat. Tonight, the woman is eating a hamburger with fries. The man is eating vegetables on a bun.

3. The couple in this apartment just had a baby. The baby cries all night. The parents take turns getting up to feed the baby. When the mother wakes up to take care of the baby, the father sleeps. Then they change roles, and the father gets up while the mother rests. They are very tired.

4. The caretaker is painting this apartment because a man has just moved out, and a new couple is moving in. He has already painted the kitchen and the bedroom. Now he is standing on a ladder and painting the living-room ceiling.

5. Two students share this apartment. They have a problem, because one student is very messy and the other is very neat. The messy student leaves her clothes all over the apartment and leaves dishes in the sink. The neat student puts everything away.

6. There is an older couple in this apartment. They have a small cat and a bird. They often watch movies on TV at night. When their grandchildren come to visit on the weekends, they go for a walk in the park. When they get home, the grandmother serves cookies and milk to the children.

7. The family in this apartment are watching TV, but they are having a fight about which show to watch. The father wants to watch sports, the mother wants to watch a movie, the daughter wants to watch a comedy, and the son wants to watch a detective show. Every few minutes, someone changes the channel.

8. The couple in this apartment are very tired. They just moved into the apartment, and there are boxes everywhere. They are unpacking their dishes and glasses in the kitchen. Tomorrow they will paint their bedroom. Then they will put their clothes in the closets.

9. There are two young children in this apartment, and there is a big dog. The children like to play with the dog, and they make a big mess. They often run in the hall, and make a lot of noise. Right now, they are jumping on their beds. The dog is jumping too.

B   Do a survey of the apartments. Read the paragraphs again and find the answers to these questions about the building.

1.   How many young children live in the building?

2.   How many families live there?

3.   How many people like to eat vegetables?

4.   How many apartments are a mess right now?

5.   How many people make a lot of noise?

6.   How many people watch a lot of TV?

7.   How many rooms are being painted this week?

8.   How many people like to cook?

9.   How many pets are there in the building?

10.   How many people like to watch movies on TV?

11.   How many couples without children live in the building?

12.   How many people are tired?

I'M CALLING ABOUT AN APARTMENT

  LISTENING ACTIVITY *2*

A   Look at the picture on page 19. Find these appliances:

1.   a dishwasher

2.   a washing machine

3.   a stove

4.   an oven

5.   a refrigerator

6.   a dryer

7.   an iron

8.   a toaster

9.   a coffee maker

10.   a blender

11.   a food processor

12.   a microwave oven

13.   an electric kettle

14.   a clock radio

CANADIAN CAPSULES

Many people keep the temperature inside their home at 19°C. People are comfortable at this temperature. If people are very active, or if they are wearing more clothes, the temperature can be a little lower.

 B   Read the questions aloud with a partner.

 C   Listen and answer the questions.

1. What is the monthly rent?

2. Which floor is the apartment on?

3. Which kitchen appliances does it have?

4. Which utilities are included?

5. What does Robert ask about next?

6. How much does indoor parking cost?

7. When is the apartment available?

Turn to page 26 for Exercise D.

WHAT IS THE RENT?

 Work with a partner. Exchange information to complete your charts.

Partner A: Use the chart on this page.

Partner B: Turn to page 27.

Partner A

Ask your partner for information to complete your chart.

Address	Rent per month	Date available
1. 7337 Birch Avenue		
2.	$635	November 1
3. 2110 Mayor Avenue		March 9
4.	$653	
5. 4236 Royal Street		April 11
6.	$745	July 1
7. 5890 Greene Crescent		
8.	$595	March 15
9. 5295 Willow Street		
10. 3615 King Street		

ROLE PLAY: FINDING AN APARTMENT

 A Work with a partner. One person is the building manager. The other person wants to rent an apartment. Write a dialogue.

 B Act out your dialogue.

CANADIAN CAPSULES

In winter, buildings and stores are kept warm, even though it is very cold outside. It is a good idea to wear layers of clothes, so you will not be too warm when you go inside.

 **Present Simple Tense: Negative**

Use **do not** (or **does not**) before the base form of the verb.

> I do not live here.
>
> He does not live here.

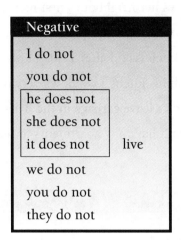

Negative	
I do not	
you do not	
he does not	
she does not	
it does not	live
we do not	
you do not	
they do not	

Contraction	
I don't	
you don't	
he doesn't	
she doesn't	
it doesn't	live
we don't	
you don't	
they don't	

A   Write the verbs in the negative. Use contractions.

1. The caretaker fixes the appliances in the kitchen.

2. Our new neighbours have a vacuum cleaner.

3. Those children make noise when they play in the lobby.

4. Kim phones a plumber for a blocked sink.

5. That man likes to live on the ground floor.

6. Janet answers the door bell every time it rings.

7. The roof leaks when it is a sunny day.

8. Jacques pays his rent directly to the landlord.

9. The Kennedy family lives next door to us.

10. Tania cleans her whole apartment every day.

11. My parents rent an apartment for $600 a month.

12. Our neighbour sings opera in the shower.

13. The musicians practise every Tuesday and Thursday.

14. Their son puts his clothes in the closet.

15. My friends visit their relatives in Italy every year.

B   Find the sentences with errors. Correct the errors.

1.   Tom **doesn't** write letters home very often.

2.   They **doesn't** know their neighbours' phone number.

3.   That plumber **doesn't** fix leaking taps very well.

4.   Maria **don't** like riding in the elevator alone.

5.   She **doesn't** knows her neighbour's first name.

6.   The caretaker **don't** answer the phone on weekends.

7.   They **don't** watch television after 11:00 at night.

8.   Mario **don't** wash his kitchen windows very often.

9.   The tenants **doesn't** leave garbage in the halls.

10.   This building **don't** have any apartments to rent.

A LEAK IN THE CEILING

 Work with a partner. Put the sentences in order to tell a story. Start with, "One day…"

1.   He calls the caretaker and reports the leak in the kitchen ceiling.

2.   When he knocks, no one comes to the door.

3.   He sees water all over the floor in the upstairs kitchen.

4.   The sink is blocked and the kitchen tap is leaking.

5.   One day Lili's husband Fred notices water coming from the kitchen ceiling.

6.   The caretaker unblocks the sink and fixes the tap.

7.   He comes downstairs and asks Lili to find the caretaker's telephone number.

8.   He goes upstairs and knocks on the neighbour's door.

9.   The caretaker takes his key and goes into the apartment upstairs.

10.   Fred remembers that the neighbours are away for the weekend.

The problem is solved.

TALK ABOUT IT

Talk about a problem in an apartment. What is the problem? How can you fix the problem?

Present Simple Tense: Questions

Use **do** or **does** before the subject. Put a question mark (?) at the end of the sentence.

A   Make the sentences into questions.

1.   Jane Simpson lives in this apartment.

2.   This building has a live-in caretaker.

3.   You pay for your own heat and electricity.

4.   You give the rent cheque to the manager.

5.   We pay the rent on the first of the month.

6.   She gets her mail from a mailbox in the lobby.

7.   Max Berg lives in apartment 1904.

8.   This apartment building has elevators.

9.   The neighbours here seem friendly.

10.   The caretaker and his wife speak English.

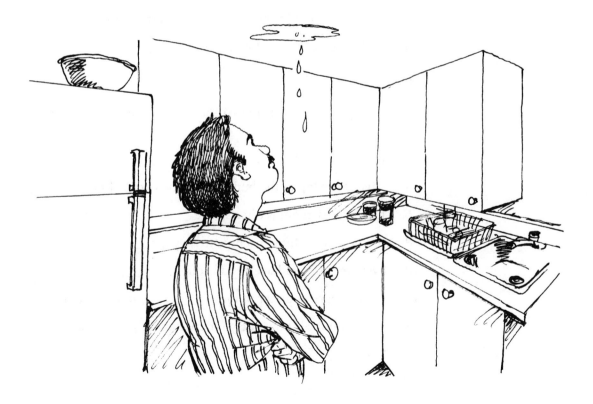

JOURNAL: WHERE I LIVE

Write about your house or apartment. Write about the building.

The Apartment Building Puzzle

Use these clues to complete the puzzle.

 Across

3. When you rent an apartment, the cost of _____ is usually not included in the rent.

5. If you have a leaky tap, you may have to call the _____.

7. The people who live near you are your _____.

9. If you live in a tall building, you use an _____ to get upstairs.

12. I live in a large building. My _____ is on the 5th floor.

13. If you have a problem in your apartment, you can call the _____.

14. The room where you sleep is called the _____.

15. Your mail is put in the _____ in the lobby.

16. At the top of the building is the _____.

Down

1. A fridge and a stove are two _____ that you need in your kitchen.

2. You cook your food in the _____.

4. I live at the top of the building, on the twenty-first _____.

6. The laundry room is often in the _____ of the building.

8. You need a washing machine to do your _____.

10. Every month you have to pay your _____.

11. You can park your car in the _____ in the building.

14. If you want to sit outside your apartment, you can sit on the _____.

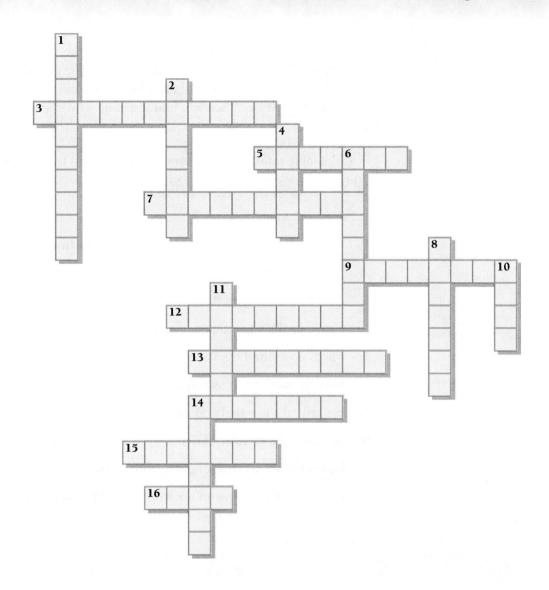

Find Someone Like You

Find people who are similar to you. Walk around the classroom and talk to the other students. First talk about yourself, to find someone who has or does similar things. When you find someone who is similar, write the student's name.

> has the same number of sisters or brothers as you have   **Pedro**
> (I have two sisters. Pedro also has two sisters.)

Find someone who:

1. has the same number of rooms in his/her apartment or house

2. gets to class the same way you do

3. likes a food that you like

4. watches a TV show that you watch

5. wakes up around the same time you do on Sunday morning

6. likes the same sport as you do

7. has visited a city that you have visited

8. has the same number of sisters or brothers as you have

9. knows the words to a song that you know

10. likes to do something on the weekends that you like to do

I'M CALLING ABOUT AN APARTMENT

LISTENING ACTIVITY 2

D   Listen and complete the dialogue. Use the worksheet.

Robert: Hello. I'm calling about the four-room apartment. What _____ the rent, please?

Manager: It's _____ a month.

Robert: What floor is it _____?

Manager: It's on the _____ floor, but there's an elevator in the building.

Robert: Is it furnished?

Manager: No, but it _____ kitchen appliances, a fridge and stove.

Robert: What about utilities? Are the heat _____ electricity included?

Manager: The heating is included, but you pay for your _____ electricity.

Robert: I see. By the way, is there _____ garage in the building?

Manager: Yes, there's an underground garage. Parking is $50 a month extra. But you _____ usually find parking on the street.

Robert: When is it available?

Manager: _____ available immediately. You can come and see it any time.

  E Work with a partner. Practise the dialogue.

WHAT IS THE RENT?

Partner B

 Ask your partner for information to complete your chart.

Address	Rent per month	Date available
1.	$660	September 16
2. 3489 Avenue Road		
3.	$750	
4. 6798 Chestnut Street		February 15
5.	$876	
6. 1838 Lorraine Crescent		
7.	$725	July 5
8. 8790 Milton Avenue		
9.	$325	April 21
10.	$495	December 18

UNIT 3
ON THE JOB

Before you start the unit, try this vocabulary quiz. Work with a partner. Choose the best answers.

1. This person works in a store.

    a) a sales clerk

    b) a secretary

    c) a hockey player

2. An orderly is someone who works in:

    a) a factory

    b) a hospital

    c) a restaurant

3. Which person works outdoors?

    a) a letter carrier

    b) a chef

    c) a pharmacist

4. Which person cuts hair?

    a) a dentist

    b) an actor

    c) a hairdresser

5. An auto mechanic works in:

    a) a barn

    b) a garage

    c)   a store

6. To get a new job, you usually have:

    a) an interview

    b) a reception

    c) a meeting

29

A   Work in a group. List all the different jobs your group can think of.

B   Copy the chart below. Put the jobs on your group's list into categories. Some jobs can be in more than one category.

Jobs

In an office _____

Outdoors _____

With food _____

In a hospital _____

In a vehicle _____

With children _____

With animals _____

At night _____

Working alone _____

C   When you finish, turn to page 39 and look at the list of jobs. Add any jobs that you missed to the categories on your group's list.

LIKES AND DISLIKES

   Look at the pictures. Where do these people work? What are their duties?

Frank   **Marian**   **Elizabeth**

B   Read about these jobs.

Frank

I'm a sales clerk in a large department store. I work in the sporting goods department. Most of the time I like my job. I like the people I work with, and I also like meeting people and helping them find the equipment they need. I didn't have any special training for my job, but I know a lot about sports. I play a lot of sports myself, so I can give people good advice on the best equipment to buy.

The thing I dislike most about my job is the pay. I only make minimum wage, and I have to work long hours. Also, the job gets boring sometimes when the store is quiet. I have to put price tags on new equipment and put things on shelves. But, all in all, I like my job. I hope to become manager of the department. Then I'll make a better salary and maybe I won't have to work on Sundays.

Marian

I'm a pharmacist in a large drugstore. When people come in with prescriptions from doctors and dentists, I fill the prescriptions. I explain to people how to take their medicine, and I also help people when they want non-prescription medications — for example, when they have a cough or a cold.

To become a pharmacist, I had to study for five years in a specialized college, and then pass an exam. My job is interesting and challenging, and the salary is good. The only thing I don't like is the hours. The pharmacy is open 24 hours a day, and sometimes I have to work all night. I get nervous when I'm alone in the pharmacy at night. But I think my job is very important, because if people don't take their medicines properly, they can become very sick. I like helping people and giving them advice and information.

Elizabeth

I'm a photographer. I take pictures for newspapers and magazines. I usually take pictures of sports and political events. I travel quite a bit because I have to be in places where important things happen. I love my job because I enjoy travelling and meeting people. Sometimes my job can be difficult or even dangerous, but most of the time it's exciting. I don't make a lot of money, but I make enough to live on. What I don't like about my job is that I'm away from home a lot. I miss my friends and my family.

To become a photographer, I took photography courses in college. Then I worked for two years for a small newspaper. Now I work on my own, and sell my pictures to different magazines and newspapers.

C Copy the chart below, and complete your chart with information from page 31.

	Frank	Marian	Elizabeth
Kind of job			
Duties			
Education or training			
Money earned			
Likes			
Dislikes			

TALK ABOUT IT

A Think of a job. It can be a job you have now, a job you had in the past, or a job you would like to have.

B Work in a group. Talk about the jobs people in the group suggest. Talk about the duties, the qualifications or training you need, and what you like and dislike about this job.

C Put the information in a chart.

Duties	Qualifications	Likes	Dislikes

CANADIAN CAPSULES

If you apply for a job in Canada, you may be asked for a résumé or CV (Curriculum Vitae). This is a document with information about your work experience and education.

I'M LOOKING FOR A JOB

LISTENING ACTIVITY 3

A Read the questions aloud with a partner.

B Listen and answer the questions.

1. What kind of job is Alex looking for?

2. Where does Tim work?

3. Why does Alex want to work there?

4. What is the pay?

5. What kind of store does Tim suggest Alex go to?

6. Why does Tim suggest Alex go there?

Turn to page 39 for Exercise C.

CANADIAN CAPSULES

The most important document a person needs when looking for work in Canada is a social insurance card, which shows the person's Social Insurance Number, or SIN. Employers are required by law to ask for this number.

GETTING A JOB

 A Read these sentences with a partner. Give your opinions. Write **T** (true) or **F** (false) for each sentence. Use your notebook.

1. It is easy to find a job.

2. You can find information about jobs in the newspaper.

3. You should not apply if a company doesn't advertise.

4. You should apply to only one place at a time.

5. Your family and friends can help you find a job.

6. At a job interview, it's acceptable to be a few minutes late.

7. You should shake hands and smile when you are greeted.

  B Read the paragraphs quickly to check your answers.

Almost everyone looks for a job at some time. Finding a job can be difficult and it can take time. If you are looking for a job, you can begin by looking in the newspaper. You can also find companies in the yellow pages of the telephone book and call them to see if they have openings. You can apply even if the companies are not advertising. Apply to as many places as possible. It is also a good idea to ask your family and friends if they know about any jobs.

If you find an opening, you will have to go for a job interview. At an interview, it is important to be prepared and to make a good impression. Always dress neatly and arrive on time. Be sure to shake hands and smile when you are greeted.

 **Comparative Adjectives**

Two different forms are used to compare two people or things.

1. Add **er** to short adjectives.

Mike is strong**er** than Bill.

2. Use **more** or **less** before adjectives with more than two syllables.

> Carla is **less** experienced than Yumi.
>
> Bill is **more** attractive than Jack.

A   Write the correct form of the adjective.

1. Basketball players are _____ (tall) than jockeys.

2. A computer is _____ (efficient) than a typewriter.

3. Students are _____ (nervous) than teachers.

4. Doctors get _____ (high) salaries than taxi drivers.

5. Some people work _____ (hard) than other people.

6. Watching a movie is _____ (enjoyable) than washing dishes.

7. The subway in New York is _____ (dangerous) than a taxi.

8. A taxi is _____ (expensive) than the bus.

9. Medical school is _____ (long) than trade school.

10. Health is _____ (important) than money.

B   Write sentences comparing these activities. Use the correct form.

1. walking to work/running to work (tiring)

2. stopping a robbery/typing a letter (exciting)

3. being an accountant/driving a taxi (profitable)

4. studying in the day/studying at night (easy)

5. washing dishes/watching TV (interesting)

6. earning money/winning money (hard)

7. finding a job/finding a mate (difficult)

8. writing a book/writing a letter (challenging)

9. eating at home/eating out (cheap)

10. driving a car/flying an airplane (complicated)

A JOB INTERVIEW

LISTENING ACTIVITY

A   Read the sentences. Then close your book and write the paragraph in your notebook as your teacher dictates it.

> Tim talks to his boss at the music store. The manager agrees to call Alex for an interview. Alex is very happy. He arrives early for his interview the next morning.

 B   Read the questions aloud with a partner.

 C   Listen and answer the questions.

1.   What kind of job is Alex applying for?
2.   Where did Alex work last year?
3.   Why didn't he like the job?
4.   What machine does Alex have to use?
5.   What evenings does Alex have to work?
6.   When does he get a pay increase?
7.   How much is the increase?
8.   What information does Alex need to give the secretary?

TALK ABOUT IT

Work in a group to discuss these questions.

Did you ever have a job interview? What happened? How did you feel? Did you get the job? What could you do better next time?

ROLE PLAY: GETTING A JOB

A   Work with a partner. Think about a job that you would like to have. If you need help, look at the list on page 39.

B   Write a dialogue about a job interview. One person works for a company that is hiring and the other person wants to get a job.

C   Act out your dialogue.

JOURNAL: A JOB I KNOW

Write about a job that you had, or about a job you would like to have. What qualifications do you need? What are the duties? What do you like or dislike about the job?

TEN-MINUTE GAMES AND ACTIVITIES

What's the Job?

Think of a job. Imagine that you have this job. On a piece of paper, write three sentences about the job. The sentences can be about the qualifications needed, the duties, the salary, the place of work, etc.

> I work in a large store.
>
> My salary is minimum wage.
>
> I help people.

Don't write the name of the job.

Put your piece of paper in a box, together with the other students' pieces of paper. Take turns pulling a piece of paper and reading the sentences to the class. All the students try to guess the job.

> Are you a sales clerk?
>
> Are you a cashier?

Job Ratings

Work in a group to rate jobs. Use the categories and jobs below. Rate each job for each category. For example, which job is the most interesting? Which job is the least interesting? Put the jobs in order from most to least. Then continue with the next category.

Try to reach a consensus in your group. Then compare your list with the results from other groups in the class.

Categories	Jobs
interesting	a police officer
difficult	a doctor
stressful	a teacher
profitable	a plumber
useful	a hairdresser
	a hockey player

Job Tic-Tac-Toe

Work in two teams, Team **X** and Team **O**.

A student from Team **X** begins by choosing a square from the grid below and making a sentence using the comparative form and any two jobs. If the comparative is used correctly, the teacher marks an **X** on the matching square on a grid on the board.

Being an musician is more interesting than being a hairdresser.

A student from Team **O** selects a square and continues in the same way. If the comparative is used correctly, the teacher marks an **O** in the square.

The first team to get three **X**s or three **O**s in a row wins. The rows can be vertical, horizontal, or diagonal.

1.

interesting	difficult	easy
profitable	useful	challenging
intelligent	stressful	complicated

2.

enjoyable	honest	smart
exciting	hard	helpful
tiring	dangerous	frustrating

I'M LOOKING FOR A JOB

 LISTENING ACTIVITY 3

 C Listen and complete the dialogue. Use the worksheet.

Tim: Hi Alex. _____ are you?

Alex: Not bad, Tim. I'm looking for a job. Are there _____ openings where you work?

Tim: I'm not sure. What kind of job are you looking _____?

Alex: Well, almost anything. I like _____ work with people, so I'm looking for a job in a store or a restaurant.

Tim: Well, _____ might need another salesperson at the music store where I work.

Alex: _____ would be great. I love music, and we could work together.

Tim: The pay _____ great, though. It's minimum wage.

Alex: Well, at least _____ a start.

Tim: OK, I'll ask _____ boss if there are any openings. Meanwhile, why don't you try the shoe store in the shopping centre? I saw a sign that said _____ were looking for a sales person.

Alex: I will. Thanks a lot for your help.

 D Practise the dialogue with a partner.

JOB LIST

an accountant	a doctor	a police officer
an actor	an engineer	a sales clerk
an artist	a hairdresser	a secretary
a bank teller	a librarian	a server
a bus driver	a musician	a shipper
a caretaker	a mechanic	a taxi driver
a computer programmer	a nurse	a teacher
a cook	a pharmacist	a truck driver
a dentist	a photographer	a window washer
a day-care worker	a plumber	a writer
a dishwasher	a pilot	a veterinarian

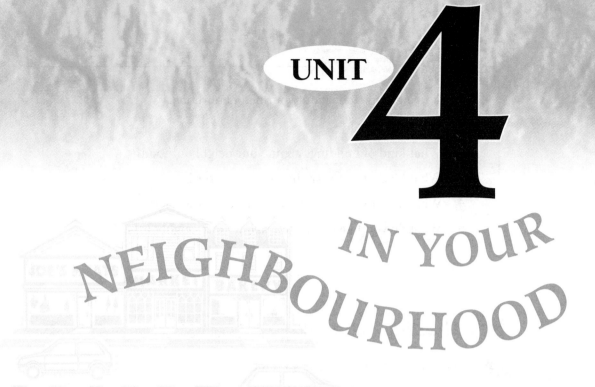

IN YOUR NEIGHBOURHOOD

QUIZ: THE NEIGHBOURHOOD

Before you start the unit, try this vocabulary quiz. Work with a partner. Choose the best answers.

1. You can usually buy postage stamps at:

    a) a supermarket

    b) a pharmacy

    c) a restaurant

2. It is safe to cross the street when the traffic light is:

    a) red

    b) yellow

    c) green

3. The person who lives next door to you is:

    a) your neighbour

    b) a stranger

    c) your relative

4. You can clean your winter coat at:

    a) the clothing store

    b) the dry-cleaner

    c) the pharmacy

5. To buy bread, you go to:

    a) a drug store

    b) a bakery

    c) a restaurant

6. You can buy a hammer and nails at:

    a) a corner store

    b) a garage

    c) a hardware store

Work in a group. Talk about your neighbourhood.

1. Where do you live?
2. What kind of buildings are in your neighbourhood?
3. What kind of stores are in your neighbourhood?
4. What kind of services are in your neighbourhood?
5. What do you like and dislike about your neighbourhood?

NEIGHBOURHOODS

A Look at the picture on page 43. Find:

a post office	a bakery	a fire hydrant
a laundromat	a convenience store	neighbours
a park	a bus stop	a bench
a bicycle	a fence	a crosswalk
a cat	a letter carrier	a dog on a leash
garbage bags	a mail box	a subway station
a supermarket	traffic lights	a dry-cleaner
a restaurant	a drugstore	a stop sign

B Use the words below to complete the paragraphs.

corner   schools   bread   city   laundromat   neighbourhoods
letter carrier   dry-cleaner   restaurants   drugstore   people

Cities have many different areas, called __1__. Each neighbourhood has its own __2__, shopping areas, churches, and sports arena. In your neighbourhood, you can get fresh __3__ in a bakery, or a newspaper at your __4__ store. You can get medicine at the __5__ near your house, wash your clothes at the __6__, or have your clothes cleaned at the __7__. And each neighbourhood has its own __8__ with special foods.

In a big __9__, you can't meet everyone. But you can meet the __10__ who work in the stores near you. You can meet the __11__ who delivers your mail. And you can meet the people who live next to you. They are your neighbours.

I'M YOUR NEW NEIGHBOUR

 LISTENING ACTIVITY 5

 A Read the questions aloud with a partner.

 B Listen and answer the questions.

1. Which apartment does Patricia live in?

2. Where is the closest post office?

3. Until what time is the supermarket open every day?

4. What can they get at the corner store?

5. What time does it close?

6. Name three things they can get at the bakery.

7. What does Patricia invite Amy for later?

Turn to page 53 for Exercise C.

WHERE CAN I FIND IT?

A Read this paragraph. Then close your book. Write the sentences as your teacher dictates.

> It's sometimes difficult to know where to buy things in a city or town. We all know that you can buy a chair in a furniture store. Did you know that you can also buy a chair in a hardware store? We all know that you can buy bread at a supermarket. Do you know other places where you can buy bread?

B Look at the list of things you sometimes need to buy. Talk about where you can buy them.

1. toothpaste
2. cookies
3. coffee
4. bread
5. aspirin
6. a paperback

7. milk
8. a newspaper
9. a dictionary
10. a birthday cake
11. stamps
12. shampoo

13. a tea kettle
14. paint
15. mugs
16. bananas
17. muffins
18. light bulbs

C   Work in pairs. Copy the chart below. Write the names of the articles in Exercise B in the places where you can find them. Then add three new things to the list for each store. Share your ideas with the class.

 Hardware store	 Convenience store	 Bakery

 Bookstore	 Supermarket	 Drugstore

TALK ABOUT IT

Work in a group. Imagine that the students in your group have just moved into your neighbourhood. Do you have a favourite restaurant, bakery, or hardware store? Give advice about the best places to get things in your neighbourhood. Use the articles from the list on page 44 to help you.

GRAMMAR FOCUS

Present Continuous

Use the present continuous for actions that are in progress now.

I'm eating an apple (right now).

Use the present continuous for temporary situations.

I'm working at the drugstore (this summer).

To form the present continuous, put the auxiliary verb **be** before the main verb. Add **ing** to the verb to show continuous action. Use **am**, **is** or **are** to show present time.

Affirmative	
I am	
you are	
he is	
she is	
it is	eating
we are	
you are	
they are	

Contraction	
I'm	
you're	
he's	
she's	
it's	eating
we're	
you're	
they're	

 A Look at the pictures on page 47. Match the questions and the answers.

1. What is the pharmacist doing?
2. What is the delivery boy doing?
3. What are the children doing?
4. What is the police officer doing?
5. What are the taxi drivers doing?
6. What is the letter carrier doing?
7. What are the servers doing?
8. What is the cashier doing?

a) They are playing ball.
b) She is stopping traffic.
c) She is delivering mail.
d) They are waiting at the corner.
e) He is riding his bicycle.
f) He's putting groceries in a box.
g) They are carrying trays.
h) She is filling prescriptions.

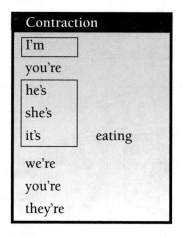
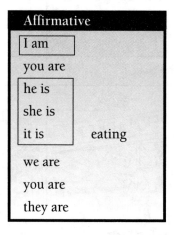

B Put the verbs in the present continuous form.

The neighbourhood is busy today. People __1_____ (do) their jobs.
The clerk in the store __2_____ (help) customers. The florist
__3_____ (sell) flowers. The cashier in the supermarket
__4_____ (put) packages in bags.

The dentist __5_____ (fix) people's teeth. The fruit seller
__6_____ (write) a sign about a sale of mangoes. A police officer
__7_____ (give) a ticket. Shoppers __8_____ (look) for
bargains. Some people __9_____ (sit) in an outdoor cafe having
coffee. The traffic __10_____ (block) the street.

48   Unit 4

TALK ABOUT IT

Discuss these questions in a group.

1.   What are some animals you see in Canadian cities?

2.   What are some animals you find in cities in other countries?

3.   Which city animals do people like?

4.   Which city animals do people dislike?

ANIMALS IN THE CITY

A   Look at the pictures. Which of these animals do you see in your neighbourhood?

B   Work with a partner. Read one paragraph and then stop. Answer the questions **orally**.

Then continue in the same way with the rest of the story.

Animals in the City

1. If you walk along any city street, before long you will probably see someone walking a dog. Dogs and cats are the most common animals in cities. They are popular indoor pets, but we often see them outside as well, on city streets and in gardens, alleys, and parks.

2. Other animals, that aren't pets, also live in cities, and they aren't always so popular. In fact, some people think these animals are pests. One example is the pigeon, a bird that we often see in parks. Pigeons are usually brown, black, blue, or grey. They live in groups and often build their homes on people's balconies or on roofs. They are noisy and they make a mess.

3. If you live near the woods or near a park, you might have animal visitors at night. Raccoons are furry animals that are bigger than cats. They have bushy tails and they look as though they are wearing masks because they have black fur around their eyes. They often come to people's houses at night to look for food. If they smell food, they turn over garbage cans or rip open garbage bags. They can leave a big mess in your yard.

4. Squirrels can also make a mess looking for food, but they are more popular because people think they are cute. They have large black eyes, round ears, and bushy tails. They are lively animals that run in trees and in parks. When people see squirrels in parks, they often like to give them food. Squirrels especially like to eat nuts. Squirrels will come up to you and take the food from your hand, but if you feed a squirrel, be careful. Even a tame squirrel can bite or scratch. Squirrels may be cute, but they are still wild animals.

Paragraph 1

1. What are the most common city animals?

2. Name four places we often see these animals.

Paragraph 2

3. Name a bird that many people think is a pest.

4. What colours are these birds?

5. Where do they build their homes?

6. Why do people dislike them?

Paragraph 3

7. What size are raccoons?

8. Why do they come to people's homes at night?

9. How do they make a big mess in the yard?

Paragraph 4

10. Why are squirrels more popular than raccoons?

11. What do people often do when they see squirrels in parks?

12. What do squirrels like to eat?

13. What will squirrels do if you feed them?

14. Why should you be careful if you feed a squirrel?

C Read the text carefully again. Write the answers to the questions.

I WAS WONDERING . . .
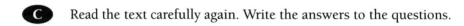
WHAT'S THE WEATHER LIKE?

LISTENING ACTIVITY 6

  A Read the questions aloud with a partner.

1. Where is Ping staying in Vancouver?

2. What are the two cousins doing?

3. What is the weather like?

4. What does Ping wonder about Vancouver?

5. In which seasons is there a lot of rain in Vancouver?

6. What is the weather like in most of Canada in the winter?

7. How is the climate in Vancouver different?

8. Does Vancouver have snow in the winter?

9. How much rain is there in Vancouver every year?

10. What does Ping decide to do?

B   Listen and answer the questions.

C   Match the expressions that mean the same thing.

1. I was wondering about…   a) gentler

2. famous   b) I understand.

3. milder   c) I was thinking about…

4. That's true.   d) That's a good idea.

5. I see.   e) well known

6. That isn't a bad idea.   f) That's correct.

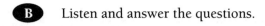
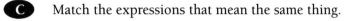

JOURNAL: MY NEIGHBOURHOOD

Imagine that a cousin from another city is thinking of moving to your neighbourhood. Write a letter to your cousin describing your neighbourhood.

Describe the stores and services and the people who live near you. Write about things you like and things you don't like about your neighbourhood.

CANADIAN CAPSULES   City animals such as pigeons and squirrels cannot be eaten. These animals may be unhealthy because they eat leftover food from people's garbage cans.

TEN-MINUTE GAMES AND ACTIVITIES

Spot the Differences

Work in pairs. Look at the two pictures. See how many differences you can find in five minutes. Use the present continuous to describe the changes.

> In Picture A the woman is wearing a coat.
> In Picture B she is wearing a sweater.

Categories

Work with a partner to put these words into categories. You should have eight categories, with three words in each group.

pigeon	corner store	juice
stop sign	milk	traffic lights
bread	mailbox	squirrel
crosswalk	grocery store	supermarket
toothpaste	post office	shampoo
cookies	coffee	muffins
aspirin	light bulbs	hammer
paint	raccoon	letter carrier

I'M YOUR NEW NEIGHBOUR

LISTENING ACTIVITY 5

  C Listen and write the words to complete the conversation. Use the worksheet.

Patricia: Hi. I'm Patricia. I just moved _____ from _____. I'm in apartment 3B.

Amy: Hi Patricia. Nice to meet you. _____ Amy. If you want to know anything about the neighbourhood, just ask. I'll be happy to help.

Patricia: Well, actually, I do have _____ few questions. I was wondering where I could find a post office.

Amy: A post office? _____ closest one is in the drugstore. It's at the corner, across from the supermarket.

Patricia: Thanks. Oh, _____ you know the hours of the supermarket?

Amy: Sure. It's open every day until 6:00, but on Thursdays _____ Fridays it's open until 9:00. If you just need a few things, milk _____ a newspaper, you can always go to the corner store. It's open until 11:00 every night.

Patricia: That's good to know. I was just going out to pick up _____ bread.

Amy: If you want fresh bread, why _____ you go to the bakery on Oak Street? They have fresh bread every day, and they have great muffins and cakes.

Patricia: What a good idea. Would you like to stop _____ for coffee and muffins later?

Amy: I'd love to. Thanks.

 D   Practise the conversation with a partner.

UNIT 5

THE FOOD WE EAT

QUIZ: FOOD

Before you start the unit, try this vocabulary quiz. Work with a partner. Choose the best answers.

1. For breakfast, Canadians often eat:

   a) soup

   b) cake

   c) eggs

2. Canadians call their evening meal:

   a) lunch

   b) brunch

   c) supper

3. In the morning, many Canadians drink:

   a) tea

   b) coffee

   c) water

4. In Canada, orange juice is a popular drink:

   a) with breakfast

   b) after dinner

   c) before bed

5. Toast is a kind of:

   a) bread

   b) cereal

   c) fruit

6. Which of these is a popular main course in Canada?

   a) rice

   b) corn

   c) chicken

NAMES OF FOODS

A   Work in a group. Make a list of all the kinds of food you can think of.

B   Copy the chart below. Put the foods into the categories on the chart.

Fruits	Vegetables	Dairy products	Meat	Fish	Cereals/breads

C   When you have finished, compare your list with another group's list.

WHAT DO YOU LIKE TO EAT?

A   Copy the chart below. Complete the chart for yourself. Write what you eat for each meal and what your favourite foods are.

B   Survey three other students. Find out what they eat and what their favourite foods are. Complete your chart.

Name				
Breakfast				
Lunch				
Supper				
Favourite: Main course				
Snack				
Fruit				
Vegetable				
Drink				
Desert				
Sandwich				

TALK ABOUT IT

Discuss these questions in a group.

1. What kinds of food do you like to eat?

2. Name three foods that you like to eat in your home.

3. Have you eaten any new foods recently? What are they?

4. Are there any new foods you would like to try?

FOODS FROM MANY LANDS

  A What do you know about food? Read these questions with a partner. Answer **T** (true) or **F** (false).

1. Ice cream is a new kind of desert.

2. Many people in Canada eat bread with every meal.

3. Ice cream comes from a cold country.

4. Coffee comes from a tree.

5. Most of the bread we eat in North America is made from wheat.

6. Ice cream was first made in Italy.

7. Coffee gives people energy.

8. People in Mexico make bread from corn.

CANADIAN CAPSULES

In different parts of Canada, people have different names for the meal at the end of the day. Some people call it "supper," and other people call it "dinner." When people eat their main meal at lunch time, they may call it "dinner" as well.

B Read all the stories quickly to check your answers to the questions on page 57.

Our Daily Bread

Bread is a basic food in Canada. Many Canadians eat bread two or three times a day. They have toast for breakfast, a sandwich for lunch, and bread and butter with their supper.

Most of the bread we eat is made from wheat, but other grains, such as oats and rye, are used to make bread too. Different countries use different grains to made bread. For example, in Mexico, corn is used to make some kinds of bread.

Many different kinds of bread are available. White sliced bread is good for toast or sandwiches. Bagels are popular for breakfast. Rolls are good to eat with lunch, and French bread is often served in restaurants.

People like to put different toppings on bread. You can spread butter, margarine, jam, or peanut butter on bread or toast, and cream cheese is a popular topping for a bagel. People often put mustard or ketchup on rolls or buns when they make sandwiches. But you don't have to put anything on bread at all. It's delicious by itself, especially when it is hot and fresh.

Many people make their lunches at home and bring them to work or class. They often bring their lunches in a brown paper bag. That is why taking your lunch to work or class is called "brown bagging."

Questions

1. How often do Canadians eat bread?
2. How do Canadians like to eat bread for the following meals?
   a) breakfast
   b) lunch
   c) supper
3. What is bread usually made from?
4. In which country is corn used to make bread?
5. What kind of bread is good for toast or sandwiches?
6. Where is French bread often served?
7. Name some toppings you can put on bread or bagels.
8. What do people often put on buns when they make sandwiches?

The Story of Ice Cream

Ice cream is one of the most popular desserts we have today. Children and adults like its cold, sweet taste. People stop for ice cream cones when they are out shopping or playing, or they bring containers of ice cream home. Dozens of flavours are available today, but vanilla and chocolate are still the most popular.

People loved ice cream right from the start, when it was invented over 4000 years ago. This delicious dish doesn't come from a cold country, as you might think; it comes from China. It was invented at the time when people there first had cows for milk, and milk was a special treat. The rulers of China had a favourite food, which they ate as a dessert. It was a dish of rice cooked with milk and spices. The rice and milk dish was put in snow to make it cold. Later, the Chinese began to mix fruit juice with the milk and rice. They sold these ice milks and ice fruits on the street as desserts.

The next people to make ice milk and fruit ice were the Italians. They had a special recipe for their desserts that was kept secret by the chefs of wealthy people. The ice desserts took a long time to make, and only rich people ate them.

Soon the French started to make frozen desserts. They added flavours such as lemon, lime, cherry, and strawberry. They also added cream to the ice desserts. This made the desserts more like our modern ice cream. Soon afterwards, the Italians learned that when they added salt, their ice cream was more solid. They sold their ice cream in the streets from carts. Italian ice cream is popular everywhere today.

Questions

1. Why do people like ice cream?

2. Which flavours are the most popular?

3. Where and when did ice cream begin?

4. What was a favourite food of the rulers of China?

5. How did people in China make their dessert cold?

6. What did they mix with the milk and rice?

7. Which people in Italy had the recipe for ice cream?

8. Name some flavours that the French added to their frozen desserts.

9. Why did the Italians add salt to their ice cream?

10. Where did the Italians sell ice cream?

Our Favourite Drink

Coffee is one of the most popular drinks in the world. You can find coffee shops on almost every corner of large cities in Canada. Many people like coffee in the morning because it helps them wake up. Coffee has caffeine in it. Caffeine gives people more energy.

Coffee comes from the seeds of a coffee plant. These seeds are called beans. The coffee beans are roasted and ground to make coffee. Coffee plants grow in hot places. They need a lot of sun and a lot of rain.

When people first discovered the coffee plant, they did not use the plant to make a drink—they ate parts of it! They chewed the berries of the plant when they travelled, to give them energy. Some people even used the leaves from the coffee plant to make wine.

Later, people started to find new ways to use coffee. They roasted and ground the beans. Then they put the beans in hot water to make a drink. The drink first became popular in Egypt and Turkey. Later, it became popular in Europe.

➡

Each country has its own way of drinking coffee. In North America, people add cream and sugar. In France, people put hot milk in their coffee. Europeans drink strong black coffee, and Italians like to add cinnamon or chocolate. Irish coffee is the strongest coffee. It has whisky in it!

Questions

1. Where can you find coffee shops?

2. Why do people like to drink coffee in the morning?

3. What are coffee beans?

4. Where do coffee plants grow?

5. What do they need to grow well?

6. Why did people eat coffee berries?

7. How did people use coffee beans later?

8. Where did the drink become popular?

9. Match the places with the ways of drinking coffee:

    1. North America   a) with whisky

    2. France   b) with cream and sugar

    3. Europe   c) with cinnamon or chocolate

    4. Italy   d) with hot milk

    5. Ireland   e) strong and black

C   Choose **one** story. Read the story carefully, and answer the questions that follow.

D   Tell your story to your group.

E   Write your story from memory.

 **Present Continuous: Negative**

Add **not** after the auxiliary verb **be**.

Negative	Contraction A	Contraction B
I am not	I'm not	Ø
you are not	you're not	you aren't
he is not	he's not	he isn't
she is not	she's not	she isn't
it is not eating	it's not eating	it isn't eating
we are not	we're not	we aren't
you are not	you're not	you aren't
they are not	they're not	they aren't

A Make the sentences negative. Use Contraction B.

1. They are having fish for dinner tonight.

2. We are going out for Chinese food this week.

3. Gina is preparing a green salad for the party.

4. Ana and Pedro are setting the table.

5. She is eating dessert after this big meal.

6. He is cooking dinner at my house.

7. Roberto is washing the dishes.

8. They are leaving the party early.

9. Ping is waiting for the bus in the rain.

10. You are helping with the cleaning up.

B These sentences are wrong. Look at the picture on page 63 and correct the information.

> A man is passing the salt.
>
> **A man isn't passing the salt. A woman is passing the salt.**

1. A young man is sitting at the end of the table.

2. A young woman is carrying chicken to the table.

3. A child is putting salad on her plate.

4. A girl is eating rice.

5. Two children are eating cookies.

6.   An older man is drinking coffee.

7.   A baby is crying.

8.   A man with a moustache is putting butter on his bread.

9.   A woman is pouring tea.

10.   An older woman is eating pie.

 **GRAMMAR FOCUS**   **Present Continuous: Questions**

Put the auxiliary verb **be** before the subject of the sentence.

| Sue is sitting in cafe. | **Is Sue sitting in a cafe?** |

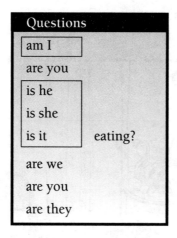

Questions

am I
are you
is he
is she
is it   eating?
are we
are you
are they

A   Change the sentences to questions.

1.   You are feeling hungry.

2.   He is waiting for someone.

3.   They are ordering tea with dinner.

4.   She is buying her groceries for the week.

5.   We are all ordering the same thing.

6.   The server is coming to take our order.

7.   You are waiting for your dessert.

8.   The server is pouring the coffee now.

9.   Some people are leaving the restaurant.

10.   It is raining very hard.

B   Write five questions in the present continuous to ask a partner.

 **CANADIAN CAPSULES**   The most popular items on menus in restaurants in Canada are french fries and soft drinks.

AN INVITATION TO DINNER

A Read this paragraph with a partner.

Elizabeth is having a pot-luck supper. At a pot-luck supper, everyone brings a different kind of food. Some people bring main courses, other people bring side dishes, and some people bring dessert. This way, everyone has good food to eat and no one has to do too much work.

 B With your partner, discuss which foods go in each category.

chicken   fish   rice   chocolate cake   apple pie   roast beef   salad
roast potatoes   ice cream   noodles   peas and carrots   cookies
lobster   green beans   shrimp   broccoli   pudding

Main course	Side dish	Dessert

 C Read the questions aloud with a partner.

D   Listen and answer the questions.

1. When is the party?

2. What kind of party is it?

3. What is Elizabeth cooking?

4. What is her sister bringing?

5. What is Bob bringing?

6. What foods does Julie ask about, after she offers to bring rice?

7. What kind of pie will Julie bring?

8. What will Elizabeth serve with dessert?

9. What time is the party?

Turn to page 71 for Exercise E.

TALK ABOUT IT

Work in pairs to plan a party. Decide on the kind of party, the date, and the locale. Then, plan the menu.

Invite other students in your class to your party. Write invitations.

SHOPPING FOR FOOD

  A   Work with a partner. Look at the pictures. Use the words under the pictures to complete the expressions.

1. a _____ of eggs	9. a _____ of milk
2. a _____ of oil	10. a _____ of tuna
3. a _____ of mayonnaise	11. a _____ of potato chips
4. a _____ of potatoes	12. a _____ of toilet paper
5. a _____ cookies	13. a _____ of juice
6. a _____ of margarine	14. a _____ of paper towels
7. a _____ of cereal	15. a _____ tissues
8. a _____ of soup	

jar   bottle   carton   can   container

bag   package   box   sack   roll

   B   Exchange information with a partner.

Partner A: Look at the information below.

Partner B: Turn to page 72.

Partner A

Look at the floor plan of the supermarket on page 68. Ask your partner where to find the foods on your list. Mark the foods on your plan. Use the worksheet.

Ask:

Where can I find… (a box of…/a can of…)

Answer:

It's beside/next to…
It's between…and…
It's to the left of/to the right of…

1. a package of cookies
2. a box of rice
3. a bottle of olive oil
4. a container of yoghurt
5. a bottle of dishwashing soap

6. a carton of orange juice
7. a box of cereal
8. a container of ice cream
9. a sack of potatoes
10. a bag of onions

Plan A

Aisle 1	Aisle 2	Aisle 3	Aisle 4	Aisle 5	Aisle 6	Aisle 7
Lettuce	Canned Soup	Tea	Laundry Detergent	Bread	Meat	Cheese
Celery	Noodles	Coffee	Pet Food	Potato Chips	Fish	Milk
Broccoli	Flour	Salad Dressing	Toilet Paper	Muffins	Chicken	Eggs
Carrots	Sugar	Peanut Butter	Tissues	Cakes	Frozen Foods	Cottage Cheese
Oranges			Paper Towels	Pies		
Bananas			Soft Drinks	Jam		
Apples						

I WAS WONDERING . . .

WHAT TIME DO YOU EAT?

LISTENING ACTIVITY 8

 A   Look at the picture. Where are the two women? What are they doing?

B Read the questions aloud with a partner.

1. Where are Danuta and Anna sitting?

2. What is Anna doing in Winnipeg?

3. What kind of people start work at nine o'clock?

4. What time does Danuta eat breakfast?

5. Do all the people in Danuta's office have lunch at the same time?

6. What does Danuta do when there is a coffee break?

7. When is the main meal in Canada?

8. When does Danuta usually make supper?

9. Why does Anna suggest they go to Danuta's place?

10. Why do they decide to cook hamburgers?

C Listen and answer the questions. Use your notebook.

D Match the expression and the meaning.

1. I'm getting hungry.   a) as early as possible after

2. to have breakfast   b) your apartment or house

3. Let's take a break.   c) to eat breakfast

4. by noon   d) They cook quickly.

5. as soon as   e) I'm beginning to feel hungry.

6. your place   f) by 12 o'clock

7. They don't take long to cook.   g) Why don't we stop work for a while?

E Work in pairs. Write a dialogue. Use the expressions in Exercise D in your dialogue.

JOURNAL: A GREAT MEAL

Write about a good meal that you had, or a meal that you would like to have, with your favourite foods.

TEN-MINUTE GAMES AND ACTIVITIES

Food Ratings

Work in a group to rate the foods. Use the categories below. Rate each food for each category. For example, which food is the most tasty? Which food is the least tasty? Put the foods in order from most to least. Then continue with the next category.

Try to reach a consensus in your group. Then compare your list with the results from other groups in the class.

Categories	Foods
tasty	a cheese sandwich
easy to make	apple pie
expensive	fried eggs
good for you	a green salad
	chocolate cake
	vegetable soup
	blueberry muffins

Quick Review

Work in teams. Answer these questions without looking back at the unit. The first team to have all the correct answers wins.

1. Which country first made ice cream 4000 years ago?
2. Name a food that comes in a can.
3. What is a pot-luck supper?
4. What do people in North America like to put in their coffee?
5. How many meals do most Canadians eat every day?
6. What is most of the bread we eat in Canada made of?
7. What kind of container do eggs come in?
8. Name three green vegetables.
9. Name three popular toppings for bread or toast.
10. What are the two most popular ice cream flavours?
11. What are two names for the meal we eat at the end of the day?
12. What kind of container does cereal come in?
13. Name two kinds of foods that we eat as a main course.
14. What are three kinds of desserts?
15. Name a food we can eat as a side dish.

AN INVITATION TO DINNER

E Listen and complete the dialogue. Use the worksheet.

Elizabeth: Hi Julie. _____ Elizabeth. I'm having some friends over for dinner on Saturday. It's a pot-luck supper. Would _____ like to come?

Julie: A pot-luck supper? What a great idea. I'd love to come. What _____ I bring?

Elizabeth: Well, let's see. I'm making _____ chicken, and my sister is bringing a big salad.

Julie: What _____ some rice?

Elizabeth: I think Bob is bringing rice and vegetables.

Julie: _____ about some bread and cheese?

Elizabeth: I think my cousin is bringing that. But we don't have _____ dessert. Would you like to bring a pie or cake?

Julie: Sure. I can make an apple pie. We can _____ it with ice cream.

Elizabeth: That sounds good. I'll serve tea _____ coffee, of course.

Julie: What time is the party?

Elizabeth: It's at 6:30.

Julie: OK. Thanks _____ inviting me!

Elizabeth: My pleasure. See you then. 'Bye.

  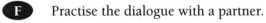

F Practise the dialogue with a partner.

SHOPPING FOR FOOD

 Partner B

Look at the floor plan of the supermarket. Give your partner information on how to find foods on his or her list. Then ask your partner where to find the foods on your list. Mark the foods on your plan. Use the worksheet.

Ask:

Where can I find… (a box of…/a can of…)

Answer:

It's beside/next to…

It's between…and…

It's to the left of/to the right of…

1. a carton of milk
2. a roll of paper towels
3. a bag of apples
4. a jar of salad dressing
5. a jar of coffee
6. a package of muffins
7. a can of soup
8. a bag of carrots
9. a bag of potato chips
10. a jar of jam

Plan B

| Lettuce / Celery / Broccoli | Onions Potatoes Oranges Bananas | | Noodles Rice Flour Sugar Cereal | Tea Oil Peanut Butter | Dishwashing Soap / Laundry Detergent / Pet Food / Toilet Paper / Tissues / Soft Drinks | Bread Cookies Cakes Pies | Meat Fish Chicken Frozen Foods | Ice Cream Cheese Yoghurt Eggs Juice Cottage Cheese |

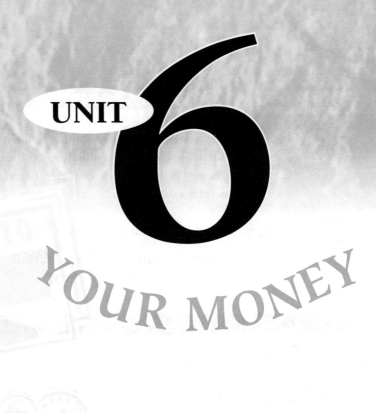

UNIT **6**

YOUR MONEY

Before you start the unit, try this vocabulary quiz. Work with a partner. Choose the best answers.

1. Which Canadian bill is coloured blue?

    a) $10

    b) $5

    c) $20

2. Canadians usually write cheques to pay:

    a) restaurant bills

    b) their rent

    c) for food

3. Which coin has maple leaves?:

    a) a penny

    b) a nickel

    c) a dime

4. A ten-cent coin is called:

    a) a penny

    b) a nickel

    c) a dime

5. The picture on a Canadian five-cent coin is:

    a) a boat

    b) a caribou

    c) a beaver

6. Which Canadian coin has a picture of a polar bear?

    a) $2

    b) a quarter

    c) $1

CANADIAN MONEY

In Canada we use two kinds of money: coins and bills. Coins are made of metal. Each coin has a picture on it. Each coin is for a different amount of money. Bills are made of paper. Each bill is a different colour. Each bill is worth a different amount of money.

  A   Work with a partner. Look at the pictures of the Canadian coins.

Copy the chart below. Then write the name and the value, and say what the picture on each one shows.

	What coin is called	Value of coin	Picture on coin

What is the picture on the back of each coin?

B Do you know which bills we have in Canada? Work with a partner. Choose from the list.

a) $1   d) $7   g) $25   j) $200

b) $2   e) $10   h) $50   k) $500

c) $5   f) $20   i) $100   l) $1000

C What colour are the different bills? Choose the colour for each bill we have in Canada.

a) purple   e) orange/brown

b) blue   f) green

c) pink   g) gold

d) orange

D What pictures are on the bills?

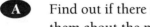

SURVEY: MONEY FROM MANY LANDS

A Find out if there are students who have money from other countries. Ask them about the money they have.

1. How many different coins do they have?

2. How many different bills do they have?

3. What is the value of their money, compared with Canadian money?

B Copy the chart below and write the information in it.

Student's countries			
Coins			
Bills			
Values			

WRITING A CHEQUE

 A Work with a partner. Look at the blank cheque below. Copy the cheque. Then make out the cheque (write in the information). Make it out to Bell Canada for $43.74. It is due on the 17th of next month.

	_____ 19___
Pay to the order of _____	$_____
Sum of _____	/100 Dollars
	_____

 B Exchange information with a partner. Use the worksheets.

Partner A: Look at the information on this page.

Partner B: Turn to page 87.

Partner A

Give your partner these instructions. He or she will fill in the cheques. Then follow the instructions your partner gives you.

1. Write a cheque to pay your rent. Make it out to Mr. Smith, for $525.00. It is due on January 1.

2. Write a cheque to pay your MasterCard bill. The amount is $187.33. It is due on November 26.

3. Make out a cheque to pay your bill at The Bay. It is for $73.46. The date is September 16.

4. You owe your friend $21.69. Write a cheque to her. Date it August 14.

The Canadian dollar coin is called a loonie because it has a picture of a loon on it. A loon is a large water bird that lives in Canada. It has bright red eyes and a strange cry.

MONEY TERMS

Match the words to the definitions.

1. a tip   a) a piece of paper you use for paying bills from your account

2. to deposit   b) an account that lets you write cheques

3. a salary   c) hourly pay from an employer

4. wages   d) to put money into the bank

5. to withdraw   e) money for good service in a restaurant

6. a chequing account   f) to take money out of the bank

7. a savings account   g) an account where you save money

8. a cheque   h) weekly or monthly pay from an employer

AT THE BANK

LISTENING ACTIVITY 9

  A Read the questions aloud with a partner.

  B Listen and answer the questions.

1. What does the customer want to do first?

2. In which account does he deposit the money?

3. What is the account number?

4. How much does he deposit?

5. What does he want to do next?

6. How much is the bill?

7. How does he pay the bill?

8. What is his chequing account number?

9. What does he have to do to his cheque?

Turn to page 87 for Exercise C.

SAVERS AND SPENDERS

A Read the story and answer the questions **orally** with a partner.

Savers and Spenders

Rose and Eddie are married. They are good friends with Sheila and Harry, who are also married. The two couples like to get together often because they have a lot of fun together. There is only one problem: money. Sheila and Harry love to spend money, but Rose and Eddie like to save.

Last Saturday night, the two couples went out for dinner. They went to a nice restaurant. Sheila and Harry ordered roast beef, with wine and desserts. Rose and Eddie wanted to save money, so they ordered salads. They drank water and they shared a small dessert. When the bill came, Sheila and Harry suggested they split the bill. Rose and Eddie were very upset. Then Sheila and Harry wanted to leave a large tip for the waiter, but Rose and Eddie wanted to leave a small tip.

Rose and Sheila often go shopping together. Sheila loves to buy new clothes and gifts for people. She goes to expensive stores, and pays with her credit card. Rose doesn't have a credit card, and she doesn't go shopping very often. She only buys things if they are on sale, and she always pays cash. She checks the newspaper every day, and waits until the stores have sales. Then she buys only what she needs.

Now the two couples have a big problem. They want to go on vacation together, but they can't decide where to go. Sheila and Harry want to go to a resort and stay in a fancy hotel. Rose and Eddie want to camp out in the woods and cook their own food. What should they do?

Questions

1. Why do the two couples like to get together?

2. What is the problem?

3. How do Sheila and Harry feel about money?

4. How do Rose and Eddie feel about money?

5. What did Sheila and Harry order in the restaurant?

6. What did Rose and Eddie order to save money?

7. Why were Rose and Eddie upset when the bill arrived?

8. What was the problem with the tip?

9. What does Sheila like to buy?

10. How does she pay for her purchases?

11. When does Rose buy things?

12. How does she pay?

13. Where do Sheila and Harry want to go on vacation?

14. What do Rose and Eddie want to do?

B Now work alone and write the answers to the questions.

 C Work in a group. Discuss what the two couples should do on their vacation.

ROLE PLAY: GETTING TOGETHER

 Work in pairs. Imagine you are friends, like Rose and Sheila. One person likes to spend money, and the other person doesn't. Decide on an activity you would like to do together. Write a funny dialogue about making plans to get together.

TALK ABOUT IT

Work in a group. Talk about these questions.

1. What do you like to spend money on?

2. What do you not like to spend money on?

3. What sorts of things do you buy on sale?

4. Do you think you are you a "saver" or a "spender"?

GRAMMAR FOCUS

Simple Past Tense: Regular

Use the simple past tense for activities completed in the past. Add **ed** to the base form of the verb to form the past tense.

> I deposit**ed** money in the bank yesterday.

Affirmative
I worked
you worked
he worked
she worked
it worked
we worked
you worked
they worked

A   Change the sentences to the past tense.

1. They visit the bank.

2. They change their money.

3. She deposits a cheque.

4. She signs the back of the cheque.

5. He waits for her to finish.

6. He opens the door for her.

7. She thanks him for holding the door.

8. They walk out of the bank together.

9. She waves for a taxi to stop.

10. They smile at each other.

CANADIAN CAPSULES   The average Canadian owns three different credit cards.

B   Choose the verb. Write it in the past tense form.

> shout   ask   cash   apologize   explain   answer   refuse
> work   count   check

Today Julio is tired. All week he __1_____ hard at his job. He __2_____ his customers' questions. He __3_____ his computer to see the customers' balances. He __4_____ out money when people __5_____ cheques.

Some customers were difficult. One woman __6_____ to sign the back of her cheque. When Julio __7_____ the bank rules, she __8_____ for the manager. Then the manager got angry and __9_____ at Julio. Later, the manager __10_____ but it was an unpleasant experience for Julio.

GRAMMAR FOCUS

Simple Past Tense: Regular—Negative

Use the auxiliary verb **did** + **not** with the base form of the main verb. The contraction of **did not** is **didn't**.

> I did not arrive late.
>
> I didn't arrive late.

Negative	
I did not	
you did not	
he did not	
she did not	
it did not	arrive
we did not	
you did not	
they did not	

Contraction	
I didn't	
you didn't	
he didn't	
she didn't	
it didn't	arrive
we didn't	
you didn't	
they didn't	

A   Write these sentences in the negative. Use the contraction.

1. The manager counted the cash after work.

2. The teller closed the bank last night.

3. The janitor opened the vault this morning.

4. The old lady cashed a cheque yesterday.

5. The student deposited money in his account.

6.   The computer worked efficiently all day.

7.   The banking machine stopped working.

8.   The new teller looked nervous.

9.   She checked the balance in her account.

10. The day seemed to be very long.

Simple Past Tense: Regular—Questions

Use the auxiliary verb **did** before the subject. Use the base form of the main verb.

You worked late.   **Did** you work late?

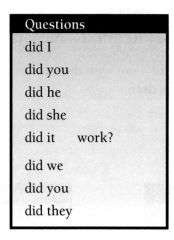

Questions
did I
did you
did he
did she
did it   work?
did we
did you
did they

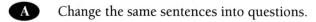 **A**   Change the same sentences into questions.

1.   The manager counted the cash after work.

2.   The teller closed the bank last night.

3.   The janitor opened the vault this morning.

4.   The old lady cashed a cheque yesterday.

5.   The student deposited money in his account.

6.   The computer worked efficiently all day.

7.   The banking machine stopped working.

8.   The new teller looked nervous.

9.   She checked the balance in her account.

10. The day seemed to be very long.

MAKING CHANGE

A   If we need to pay $20, we can use a $20 bill, two $10 bills, or four $5 bills. Write two combinations of bills you can use to make these amounts of money.

1. $22
2. $56
3. $49
4. $86

5. $32
6. $51
7. $38
8. $55

B   If we need to pay 75 cents, we can use three quarters, seven dimes and a nickel, or other combinations. Write two different combinations for these amounts of money.

1. 61 cents
2. 39 cents
3. 46 cents
4. 78 cents

5. 21 cents
6. 8 cents
7. 41 cents
8. 92 cents

I WAS WONDERING . . .

HOW DO YOU USE A BANKING MACHINE?

LISTENING ACTIVITY 10

 A   Read the questions with a partner.

B   Listen and answer the questions.

1. Where is Pedro staying in Ottawa?

2. What does he ask Bob to help him do?

3. What does Bob say about using the banking machine?

4. Where are the instructions?

5. What problem does Pedro have at first?

6. What caused the problem?

7. What does the screen say?

8. What is a P.I.N.?

9. When is the machine especially handy?

C   Answer the questions about the expressions.

1. Which three expressions mean "not difficult"?

2. Which expression means "I think" or "I imagine"?

3. Which expression describes a problem with the bank card?

4. Which expression means "It is very convenient"?

a) It's easy as pie.

b) I guess…

c) It's simple.

d) It won't go in.

e) There's nothing to it.

f) It is really handy.

JOURNAL: HOW I SPEND MY MONEY

Write about your spending habits and the way you feel about money.

CANADIAN CAPSULES

In general, Canadians are careful with their money. They save more money than Americans do.

The Money Puzzle

Use the clues to complete the puzzle. Then find the hidden words.

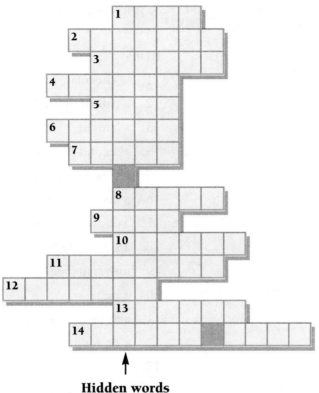

Hidden words

1. the colour of a five-dollar bill
2. the name of a 25-cent coin
3. Working people pay the government _____ tax every year.
4. the name of a 5-cent coin
5. the name of a 10-cent coin
6. the name of the Canadian dollar coin
7. the hourly pay you earn
8. the kind of leaf on the penny
9. You can charge something, or pay _____.
10. a piece of paper you can use to pay a bill from your account
11. to take money out of the bank
12. to put money into the bank
13. A P.I.N. is a personal identification _____.
14. If you don't have cash or a cheque book, you can pay for things you buy with a _____.

Using a _____ makes it easy to put money in the bank or take it out.

What Does It Cost?

 Work with a partner. Talk about the items on the list. What do you think each of the items on the list costs? Put the items into categories. If you don't think the exact price is listed, choose the closest category. Some words can go in more than one category. Compare your list with other students' lists. After class, you can go out and check the prices on some of these items.

Prices	Items
5¢	1. a chocolate bar
$1.50	2. a pair of ice skates
$5	3. a haircut
$25	4. a second-hand car
$50	5. a meal for two in a good restaurant
$150	6. a taxi ride to the airport, from downtown
$500	7. a pocket camera
$5000	8. a subway fare
$15000	9. university fees for one year
$150 000	10. a pizza
	11. a three-minute long-distance call in Canada
	12. a tip for a waiter
	13. a newspaper
	14. a pair of gloves
	15. a sweater
	16. a piece of candy
	17. a refrigerator
	18. a litre of milk
	19. a new car
	20. a winter coat
	21. a new house
	22. a couch
	23. a cup of coffee
	24. a television set
	25. an eraser

AT THE BANK

LISTENING ACTIVITY 9

C   Listen and complete the dialogue. Use the worksheet.

Teller: Yes, sir. _____ I help you?

Customer: Yes. I'd like to deposit _____ cheque in my account.

Teller: _____ this a chequing or a savings account?

Customer: _____ a savings account. My account number is 67795.

Teller: OK, _____ 67795, and the amount is $50. Is there anything else you would like to _____?

Customer: Yes, I'd also like to _____ my phone bill.

Teller: OK, the bill is for $37.50. How _____ you want to pay this?

Customer: From my chequing account, please. The number is 761-304-5.

Teller: That's fine. Please sign the back of this cheque. Anything _____?

Customer: No, that's all _____ today, thanks.

Teller: Have a nice day.

    D   Practise the dialogue with a partner.

WRITING A CHEQUE

   Partner B

Write the cheques your partner describes. Then give your partner these instructions.

1.   Write a cheque to pay your bill at Eaton's. It is for $35.99. It is due April 3.

2.   You owe your brother $16.86. Pay him on May 12.

3.   You have to pay your Visa bill. Make out a cheque for $138.98. It is due on October 29.

4.   You must pay your income tax. Write a cheque to the Receiver General of Canada (the Government of Canada) for $256.88. It must by paid by April 30.

SHOPPING

QUIZ: GOING SHOPPING

Before you start the unit, try this vocabulary quiz. Work with a partner. Choose the best answer.

1. To buy towels in a department store, go to:

    a) the clothing department

    b) the linen department

    c) the appliance department

2. The appliance department is a good place to buy:

    a) a pair of skis

    b) a refrigerator

    c) an arm chair

3. To find the price of an item, check the:

    a) label

    b) price tag

    c) collar

4. You cannot return items in a department store without:

    a) a receipt

    b) a cash register

    c) an ID card

5. Most stores in Canada have sales:

    a) every day

    b) once a year

    c) a few times a year

6. Winter coats are on sale:

    a) in the fall

    b) in January

    c) in early spring

TALK ABOUT IT

Work in a group to discuss these questions.

1. Do you know the names of any department stores in Canada?

2. Do you know the names of any department stores in other countries?

3. Do you prefer to shop in department stores or in smaller stores? Why?

4. Do you think things are more expensive in department stores or in smaller stores?

5. Where is clothing more expensive, in Canada or in other countries?

THE DEPARTMENT STORE

Work with a partner. Look at the picture of the department store on page 91. Write the names of the departments where you can find each item.

1. a winter jacket
2. a refrigerator
3. a man's suit
4. a radio
5. a gift for a new baby
6. a lamp
7. a tennis racket
8. a dress for a party
9. beach towels
10. a compact disk
11. a hammer and nails
12. an umbrella
13. a tie
14. a Father's Day gift
15. a sweater
16. a Mother's Day gift
17. a washing machine
18. a bed
19. winter boots
20. a tent for camping

CANADIAN CAPSULES

A good way to find out what people in Canada wear to work or school is to look at advertisements in major newspapers. You can also find out what kinds of clothes to wear in different seasons, and how much the clothes cost.

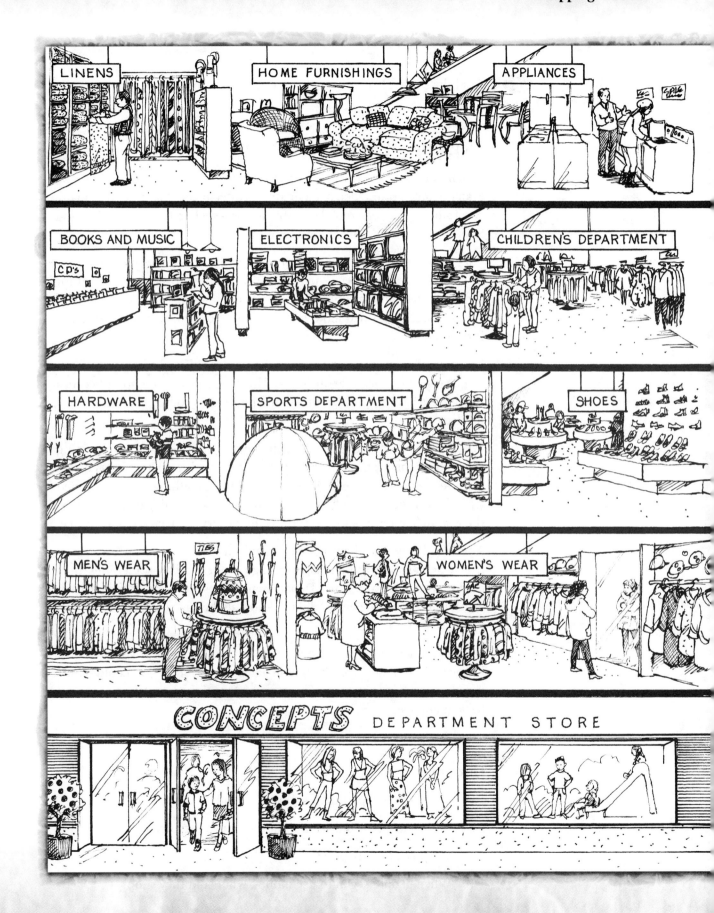

DEPARTMENT STORES IN CANADA

 A Read the story. Then answer the questions that follow.

Department Stores in Canada

When you shop for furniture or clothes in Canada, where do you go? Many people go to a department store. A department store is like many small stores under one roof. Department stores such as Eaton's, The Bay, and Sears have been in Canada for a long time.

Long ago, people traded with each other to get the clothes and food they needed. In Canada, special places, called trading posts, were set up for trading. Later, when people began to use money, they shopped in general stores. These stores had food, clothing, fabric to make clothes, tools, and furniture.

When cities grew bigger, the stores got bigger too. They had separate areas, or departments, for different items. The customers were happy, because they didn't have to walk to many different stores to buy the things they needed.

When department stores opened in Canada, people's way of shopping changed. In the past, at a trading post or a general store, there was no set price for items. When people wanted to buy something, they bargained with the owner and tried to pay the lowest price. In department stores, there were fixed prices for everything, and everyone paid the same price.

Another change was the way people paid. In general stores, people knew the owners. If they did not have enough money to buy something, they could pay a little at a time. Department stores were much bigger than general stores, and the owner did not know all the customers. Everyone had to pay cash, right away.

The department store was different in another way, too. If you were not happy with something you bought in a department store, you could return it and get your money back. This was the first time people had a money-back guarantee.

Questions

1. Name some department stores in Canada.

2. In the past, how did people get the things they needed?

3. What is a trading post?

4. When people began to use money, where did they shop?

5.   Name some items you could buy in a general store.

6.   When did stores become bigger?

7.   What are departments?

8.   Why do customers like to shop in department stores?

9.   How did people decide on a price in the past?

10.   What was different about prices in a department store?

11.   What happened if people did not have enough money in a general store? Why?

12.   How did people have to pay for items in department stores?

13.   What guarantee did the department store give?

B   After you answer the questions, check what you have written with a partner.

BUYING A WINTER JACKET

LISTENING ACTIVITY 11

A   Work with a partner. Look at the pictures of the coat and jacket. Match the words to the pictures.

   **coat   jacket   sleeves   collar   zipper   pockets   buttons
   label   price tag**

B   Read the questions aloud with a partner.

C   Listen and answer the questions.

1. Why does Laurie want to go to the clothing department?
2. What two problems does Laurie have with her old jacket?
3. What two problems does she have with the sweater?
4. What does she see next?
5. What two features does the jacket have?
6. Why will the jacket be warm?
7. What two things does she check to see if it fits?
8. What do they find that matches the jacket?
9. Where does Marla go to try on the sweater?
10. Why does Laurie want to line up at the cash right away?

Turn to page 102 for Exercise D.

PAY AT THE CASH

Read the story. Use the words listed to complete the paragraphs.

cash
steal
area
buy

A department store sells many different items, and each department has its own __1_____ and its own __2_____ register. You pay for the things you buy at the nearest cash register. It is not a good idea to walk around the store with something you want to __3_____. Someone might think that you want to __4_____ it.

cashier
receipt
people
bag

If there are a lot of __5_____ waiting to pay, you have to line up and wait for your turn. When you pay, the __6_____ puts your purchases in a __7_____, and gives you a __8_____ to show that you paid.

money
card
item
sales

You can pay cash or use a credit __9_____ or a debit card. Be sure to keep your receipt, or __10_____ slip. If there is a problem with the __11_____ you bought, or if you change your mind later, you can return the item with the sales slip, and get your __12_____ back.

Simple Past Tense: Irregular

Many common verbs in English have an irregular form in the past tense.

bring	brought
buy	bought
come	came
do	did
drink	drank
eat	ate
get	got
meet	met
sell	sold
sit	sat
sleep	slept
stand	stood
take	took
wear	wore
write	wrote

 Use the chart above. Change the sentences to the past tense.

1. He buys his clothes in the Men's Department.
2. She usually gets her shoes on sale.
3. The shopping trip takes a long time.
4. The clerk writes the price on the tag.
5. People stand in line for the sale.
6. They bring their purchases home in a bag.
7. We meet our friends at the store.
8. I eat well before going shopping.
9. He sits down to try on shoes.
10. They sleep well after shopping all day.
11. Some shoppers wear their new clothes home.
12. That store sells clothes for children.
13. The cashier does a lot of work.
14. We drink coffee for a few minutes.
15. Many people come to the sale.

begin	began
cost	cost
drive	drove
give	gave
go	went
know	knew
leave	left
make	made
put	put
say	said
see	saw
speak	spoke
tell	told
think	thought

B   Use the verbs to complete the story. Use the past tense.

think
go
see
begin
cost

One day Kelly __1_____ downtown. She looked in a store and
__2_____ a beautiful pair of shoes. The problem was that they
__3_____ too much. She __4_____ to dream about the shoes.
She __5_____ about them all the time.

tell
know
speak
give

Kelly __6_____ that her friend Paula was a good shopper. She
__7_____ to her about the shoes. She __8_____ Paula that she
loved the shoes. Paula __9_____ her a good idea: the same shoes
were cheaper at the mall.

say
put
make
leave
drive

Kelly __10_____ a decision. She __11_____ she had a headache
and __12_____ work early. She __13_____ to the mall and bought
the shoes. When she __14_____ them on, her headache went away.

BUYING ON SALE

A Look at the picture. Work with a partner. What do you think the people are doing? Why?

B Read and discuss the sentences with a partner. Do you think they are true or false? Write **T** (true) or **F** (false).

1. In Canada you can ask for a lower price in a department store.

2. Most stores in Canada have sales only once a year.

3. You can find out about sales in the newspaper or in advertising flyers.

4. Stores usually have sales at the end of the season.

5. A good time to buy a winter coat is in October or November.

6. If something is on sale, it's always a good idea to buy it.

7. You cannot return something you buy on sale.

8. You can save a lot of money by buying things on sale.

C Read the text quickly to check your answers for Exercise B.

Buying on Sale

When you buy things in other countries, do you bargain for the best price? In Canada, you generally can't bargain for a better price, especially in a department store. Instead, Canadians "look for bargains." This means they try to find the best price for something they want to buy. For example, if they need a new coat, they go to a few stores and look at the prices before they decide what to buy.

Stores in Canada have sales a few times a year. When they have sales, the prices are lower. You can find out about sales in the newspaper or from advertising flyers. By watching the ads, a smart shopper can save a lot of money by buying things on sale.

Stores usually have sales at the end of the season. They reduce the prices at the end of the season to make room for new merchandise. For example, in January, all the winter clothes go on sale. You can buy a winter coat for much less money than it would cost in September or October. This is the same for summer clothes. Bathing suits usually go on sale in June or July.

Stores have sales at other times as well—after holidays or for the store's anniversary, for example. Sometimes they have clearance sales. A store buys a big stock of certain items, such as raincoats in the spring or sheets and towels in January. Then the store puts the items on sale so they will sell quickly.

When you buy on sale you have to be careful. Just because an item is on sale does not mean that it is a bargain. Be sure that it is something you really need, and be sure to check it carefully. Before you buy it, ask yourself why it is on sale. Perhaps it is damaged or out of style. Usually you cannot return something that you buy on sale. If this is the case, the cashier will write "Final sale" on the sales slip.

D Work with a partner. Answer the questions orally. Don't write the answers.

1. What does it mean to "look for a bargain"? Give an example.

2. Where can you find out about sales?

3. Why do stores reduce prices at the end of the season?

4. What is a clearance sale?

5. What should you check before you buy something on sale?

6. What does "Final sale" mean?

E Work alone. Write the answers to the questions in Exercise D.

I WAS WONDERING . . .
WHERE CAN I BUY A SWEATER ON SALE?

LISTENING ACTIVITY 12

A   Read the questions aloud with a partner.

B   Listen and answer the questions.

1.   What does Min Hee ask Jun about?

2.   What kind of sweater does she need?

3.   What does Min Hee say about the price of the sweater?

4.   Why is it a good time of year to shop for a warm winter sweater?

5.   How do stores try to attract customers?

6.   Why do stores need room when the seasons change?

7.   Where does Jun suggest they shop?

8.   Which department does Min Hee suggest?

9.   Where does Jun think they should start?

C   Match the expressions to their meanings.

1. cheap	a)	sale of clothing for cold weather
2. winter sale	b)	Wait a minute.
3. Hold it.	c)	at reduced prices
4. on sale	d)	inexpensive

JOURNAL: GOING SHOPPING

Write about your shopping experiences. Do you like to shop? How often do you shop? What stores do you like to shop in?

TEN-MINUTE GAMES AND ACTIVITIES

Spot the Differences

Work in pairs. Look at the pictures. How many differences can you find?

A Shopping Survey

Work in a group. Ask each person in the group these questions to complete your chart. You can use the worksheet.

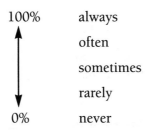

100% always

often

sometimes

rarely

0% never

	Student A	Student B	Student C
How often do you:			
1. buy something in the first store you go into?			
2. pay for clothes with a credit card?			
3. shop for more than four hours in one day?			
4. go to garage sales?			
5. read advertising fliers to look for sales?			
6. buy clothes in a department store?			
7. shop with a friend?			
8. shop alone?			
9. bring your own bags with you when you shop?			
10. buy something you don't really need, because it's on sale?			

BUYING A WINTER JACKET

LISTENING ACTIVITY 11

 D Listen and write the words. Use the worksheet.

Laurie: Marla, let's go to the clothing department. I need _____ new winter jacket. My old one is too tight, and it has a hole in the sleeve.

Marla: OK, Laurie. I need a few things _____. Hey, look at this sweater. I really like the pattern. What _____ you think?

Laurie: I'm not _____. The colour isn't that great, and it looks like it's too small.

Marla: Yeah, I guess you're right. Oh, look at this shirt. I love the colour, and it's my size.

Laurie: That's really nice. Why don't you try it _____?

Marla: I think I will. _____ about you? Did you find a jacket that you like?

Laurie: Yes, I really like this plaid _____. Look, it has lots of pockets, and it even has a hood. It's made of wool, so it should be really warm.

Marla: Why don't you try it on? _____ a big mirror over there.

Laurie: The sleeves are long enough, and the length is good too.

Marla: It looks great on you. I think you should get it. Oh look, _____ scarf matches perfectly.

Laurie: You're right Marla. It's just what I need. Why _____ you go to the fitting room and try on your shirt? There are a lot of people at the cash, so _____ get in line right away.

 E Practise the conversation with a partner.

CANADIAN CAPSULES

In some elementary and high schools in Canada, students wear uniform or have a dress code. In other schools, and in colleges and universities, students wear what they like. Most students of all ages like to wear jeans, T-shirts, and sweatshirts to school.

UNIT **8**

TRAVEL IN CANADA

QUIZ: CANADA

Before you start the unit, try this vocabulary quiz. Work with a partner. Choose the best answers.

1. Which Canadian province is on the Pacific Ocean?

   a) Nova Scotia

   b) Prince Edward Island

   c) British Columbia

2. Where is Newfoundland located?

   a) on the east coast

   b) in central Canada

   c) on the west coast

3. Which Canadian province touches Hudson Bay?

   a) Alberta

   b) Manitoba

   c) Saskatchewan

4. Which major city is nearest to Ottawa?

   a) Toronto

   b) Vancouver

   c) Montreal

5. This province borders on Quebec in the east.

   a) Ontario

   b) Manitoba

   c) New Brunswick

6. Which territory is north of British Columbia?

   a) the Northwest Territories

   b) Nunavut

   c) the Yukon

PROVINCES AND CITIES

 A   Do you know the Canadian provinces and territories? Put these letters in the correct order to find the provinces. Then locate the provinces on the map at the beginning of the book on page viii.

1. B S T I R H I   C I M B O L U A

2. M N A I T B A O

3. Q B E U C E

4. O T N A O I R

5. N V O A   S C O I A T

6. N W F O D L E U N A D N

7. Y U O K N

8. P E R C I N   E W D A D R   I S L D N A

9. S W A K A S A T H E N C

10. N W O E R T S H T   T R O R I E R I S E T

11. A B L R E A T

12. N W E   B C N R U S W K I

13. N A V U T U N

B   Match the provinces with their capital cities.

1.	British Columbia	a)	Halifax
2.	Alberta	b)	Regina
3.	Saskatchewan	c)	Edmonton
4.	Manitoba	d)	Charlottetown
5.	Ontario	e)	St. John's
6.	Quebec	f)	Fredericton
7.	New Brunswick	g)	Quebec City
8.	Nova Scotia	h)	Toronto
9.	Prince Edward Island	i)	Victoria
10.	Newfoundland	j)	Winnipeg

WHERE PEOPLE LIVE

Complete the paragraph with the words below.

cities   eastern   traffic   population   country   train

Canada is a big country with a small __1_____. Most of the major __2_____ in Canada are near the American border. In other parts of the __3_____, cities and town are far from each other. The biggest concentration of population is in __4_____ Canada between the cities of Windsor and Quebec City. The two largest cities in Canada are in this area. Bus and __5_____ services connect cities such as Toronto and Montreal. Because there is so much __6_____ between cities and towns in this part of the country, the area is sometimes called the Quebec-Windsor corridor.

TALK ABOUT IT

Work in a group. Choose two cities to discuss: one city in Canada and one city in another country. Discuss these questions to compare the cities.

1. Are the cities crowded?

2. What kind of transportation do the cities have?

3. How crowded are the main streets on Saturday night?

4. How often do you meet someone you know in a crowded place?

5. How many students are there in a high-school class?

6. How do people act while waiting for a bus?

7. Name some places where you have to line up or wait for services.

CANADIAN CAPSULES

Every year millions of people visit Niagara Falls. They are impressed by the incredible volume of water that pours over the falls—168 000 cubic meters of water every minute!

DISTANCES IN CANADA

 Work with a partner to exchange information.

Partner A: Look at the map on this page.

Partner B: Turn to page 117.

Partner A

Look at your map of Canada. It shows the distances between some cities. Ask your partner for the information that you are missing. Write it on the map. Then give your partner the information you have. Use the worksheet.

Ask: What is the distance between Winnipeg and Toronto?

Say: The distance between Winnipeg and Ottawa is 2218 kilometres.

Map A

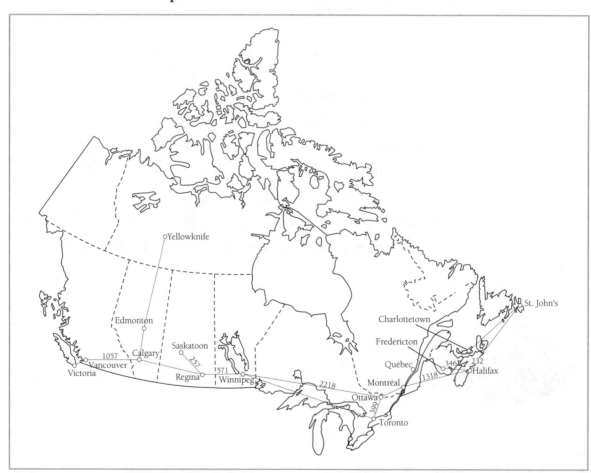

WELCOME TO VIA

LISTENING ACTIVITY 13

 Listen to the information. Answer the questions. Use the worksheet.

1. What do you need in order to take advantage of Via's automatic information service?

2. Which number should you press for schedules?

3. Give the numbers that you should press for the following cities.

    a) Toronto   b) Ottawa   c) Quebec

4. What kind of information will you get if you press 6?

5. What number do you press to hear information about the schedule for Saturday?

6. What information do you get if you press 3?

7. What number do you press to hear information about the schedule for Dorval Station?

8. If you press 0, what information will you hear?

9. Complete the chart.

Trains from Montreal to Toronto			
Depart	7:15 a.m.	Arrive	12:05 p.m.
Depart		Arrive	3:49 p.m.
Depart	2:15 p.m.	Arrive	
Depart		Arrive	10:28 p.m.

10. What number do you press to hear information about coach fares?

11. How much can you save by travelling on off-peak days?

12. How many days in advance do you have to get your tickets for off-peak fares?

13. Why is it a good idea to get your tickets early?

14. Complete the chart.

Full coach fares		Off-peak coach fares	
Adults	$72	Adults	$
Seniors and students	$	Seniors and students	$36
Children 2 to 11	$36	Children 2 to 11	$

15. What is not included in the fare?

ON VACATION

A   Look at the pictures. Work with a partner. Which adjectives describe the places?

new   old   big   small   exciting   busy   beautiful   romantic
rainy   hot   cold   windy   quiet   interesting   snowy

1. Banff National Park   5. Prince Edward Island
2. Montreal   6. Toronto
3. Niagara Falls   7. Vancouver
4. Ottawa

B Read the paragraphs. Give the name of each place.

1. This city, located in Ontario, is one of the most beautiful in Canada. People skate on the Rideau Canal in winter and come to see the tulip festival in spring. It is the site of two universities and many museums. Most important, it is the nation's capital. The parliament buildings and the prime minister's residence are here.

2. Tourists from all over the world come to visit this famous national park and see its spectacular beauty. People come to ski and hike in the high mountains and camp in the park. It is well known for the many animals, such as bear and deer, that live there. It has many hotels and ski resorts. This world-famous resort is located in the Rockies.

3. This large, modern city is the centre of industry and commerce as well as culture and the arts. It is a multicultural city; the people who live here come from all parts of the world. It is the largest city in Canada and the capital city of its province. It is on the waterfront near the western end of Lake Ontario. Two of its famous landmarks are the CN Tower and the Skydome.

4. This province is the smallest in Canada, but it is big on tourism. In fact, more than 800 000 tourists visit the province each year. Most of the tourists visit the beaches and heritage sights in the summer months, when the weather is warm. This province is an island. It is known worldwide for the stories of Anne of Green Gables.

5. A mixture of languages and cultures makes this city a popular vacation destination for people from North America and Europe. Visitors can watch sports events from baseball to hockey, eat in many wonderful restaurants, and shop in underground malls without going outside. The mountain in the middle of the city is a great place for winter sports such as skating and skiing.

6. This attractive city is a mixture of old and new. It has North America's second largest Chinatown (after San Francisco), and is a centre for cultural activities such as theatre, dance, and opera. Sandy beaches and tall mountains nearby make this city a great place for recreation and sports. Its many parks, including famous Stanley Park, have forests and a wide variety of wildlife. Its mild climate attracts visitors all year long.

7. This is one of the greatest tourist attractions of the world. Each year 12 to 15 million visitors come to see this spectacular waterfall on the border between Canada and the United States. People can view the falls from a tower or from a boat. There are many hotels in this region, which is a popular honeymoon spot.

C   Work with a partner. Answer **T** (true) or **F** (false). Correct information that is false.

1. The city with the tulip festival is the capital of Canada.

2. The smallest province in Canada is an island.

3. The largest city in Canada has a mountain in the middle.

4. The city with underground shopping has a famous waterfall.

5. People from many countries live in the city with the CN Tower.

6. The place that is a honeymoon spot has a famous waterfall.

7. The city where people skate on a canal is the capital of a province.

8. The city that has a mild climate has a large Chinatown.

9. People who go to this resort can see wild animals.

TALK ABOUT IT

Work in a group. Talk about a trip you would like to take in Canada. Why would you like to go there? What would you like to do there?

Simple Past Tense: Irregular—Negative

Regular and irregular past tense verbs form the negative in the same way. The auxiliary verb **did** means past time, and **not** signals negation. The main verb is always in the base form. The contraction of **did not** is **didn't**.

I walk**ed**.	I **did** not walk.
I drove.	I **did** not drive.

Negative		Contraction	
I did not		I didn't	
you did not		you didn't	
he did not		he didn't	
she did not	drive	she didn't	drive
it did not		it didn't	
we did not		we didn't	
you did not		you didn't	
they did not		they didn't	

A   Match the base form to the irregular affirmative form of the past tense.

1.	leave	a)	rode
2.	sit	b)	rang
3.	drive	c)	told
4.	stand	d)	got off
5.	make	e)	saw
6.	speak	f)	made
7.	know	g)	drove
8.	get off	h)	left
9.	ride	i)	met
10.	see	j)	stood
11.	hear	k)	heard
12.	ring	l)	knew
13.	meet	m)	spoke
14.	go	n)	sat
15.	tell	o)	went

B   Put the sentences in the negative form. Use contractions.

1. The bus we took yesterday left early.
2. The bus driver drove quickly.
3. The driver knew all the passengers.
4. She rang the bell to get off the bus.
5. He saw a boy running for the bus.
6. The driver spoke to the man behind him.
7. You rode your bicycle to work yesterday.
8. We heard the announcement of our flight.
9. Those people stood in line for an hour.
10. They made a mistake with our tickets.
11. I got off at the last bus stop.
12. They sat at the front of the bus.
13. We met interesting people on our trip.
14. She went to Toronto by train.
15. The travel agent told us to arrive at the airport early.

 **Simple Past Tense: Irregular—Questions**

Use the auxiliary verb **did** before the subject. Use the base form of the main verb.

> She spoke English. **Did** she **speak** English?

did I
did you
did he
did she
did it   speak?
did we
did you
did they

 Change the sentences to questions.

1. He told us to turn right at the corner.

2. The group needed a map of the city.

3. Robert lost his wallet on the tour.

4. The tour guide knew our names.

5. The bus driver made a left turn.

6. The airplane tickets cost a lot.

7. The train stopped twice on the way.

8. The guide spoke three languages.

9. We left our passports at the hotel.

10. He put all the suitcases on the bus.

11. The police found Robert's wallet.

12. She said "Goodbye" at the end of the trip.

13. The train left the station on time.

14. You wanted to stay there longer.

15. The tourists turned the wrong way.

I WAS WONDERING . . .
WHERE SHOULD WE GO?

LISTENING ACTIVITY 14

    A   Read the questions aloud with a partner.

    B   Listen and answer the questions.

1. Where did Yumi just arrive?

2. What are Keiko and Yumi talking about?

3. Where does Yumi suggest they visit?

4. What does Keiko say?

5. When does Yumi think they can go to PEI?

6. Which two places does Keiko suggest?

7. How long is the train trip to Quebec City?

8. How would they travel from Toronto to Niagara Falls?

9. What does Yumi want to see in Toronto?

C   Match the expressions and the meanings.

1. Forget it.   a) to spend the night
2. That's out of the question.   b) to make reservations
3. on our next break   c) It seems like a good idea.
4. It's pretty far.   d) It's impossible.
5. to book (a tour)   e) That's a bad idea.
6. to stay over   f) when we have a holiday
7. It sounds good.   g) It's quite a distance.

D   Work with a partner. Write a dialogue about traveling in Canada. Use the expressions above.

JOURNAL: A GREAT VACATION

Write about a great vacation that you took or about a place you would like to visit. Write about what you did, or what you would like to do.

TEN-MINUTE GAMES AND ACTIVITIES

The Canada Puzzle

Use these clues to complete the puzzle.

 Across

2. the capital of Northwest Territories
4. A bay in the north of Canada
5. a city in Alberta
7. a province in the east of Canada that is an island
11. the capital of Nova Scotia
12. the province between Ontario and Saskatchewan
15. the capital of British Columbia
16. the ocean to the north of Canada
19. the ocean to the west of Canada
22. the province between Alberta and Manitoba
23. the largest city in Canada
24. the capital of New Brunswick

 Down

1. a new territory in Canada
3. a large city in Quebec
6. the capital of Prince Edward Island
7. a famous waterfall in Ontario
8. Toronto is in this province
9. the ocean to the east of Canada
10. a territory in the northwest of Canada
13. the capital of Manitoba
14. a large city in British Columbia
17. a province in the east of Canada
18. the capital of Alberta
20. the province that is east of British Columbia
21. the capital of Canada

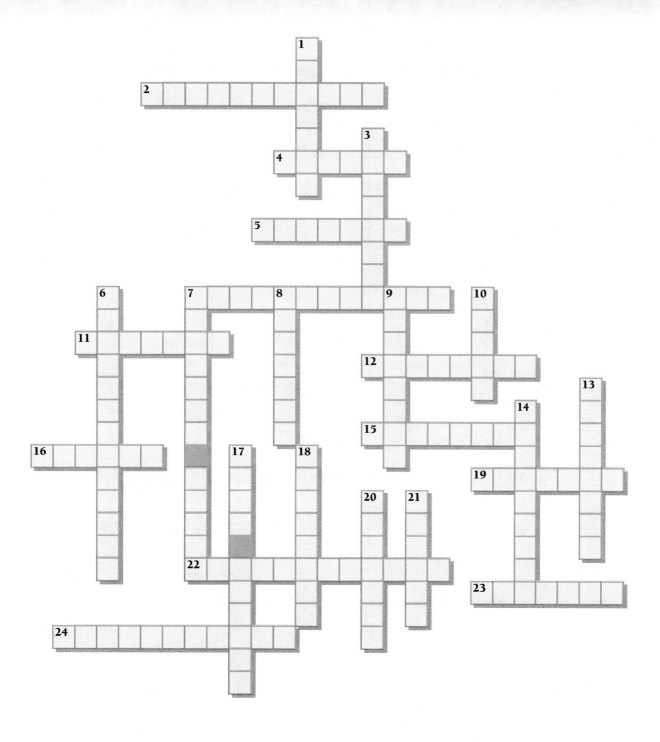

Opposites

Each word in Box A has an opposite in Box B. Find the opposites.

Box A

give   east   near

together

warmest

get on

arrive

cold

summer

above

north

true   cheap

long

biggest

wonderful

begin

rainy

early

beautiful

lose

right

best

exciting

famous

inside   ask

Box A

worst   short

hot

expensive   alone

end   terrible

outside

ugly   take

unknown

far

south   smallest

left

coolest

west

get off

late   below

find   winter

boring   dry

leave

false   answer

CANADIAN CAPSULES

Transportation in the city can be difficult when there are many cars on the road. It is even more difficult in winter, when there is ice and snow on the ground. Canadians have learned to cope with bad weather conditions. Streets are cleaned very quickly after a snow storm, and most of the time people get to work or school with few problems.

Partner B

Look at your map of Canadian cities. It shows the distances between some cities. Give your partner the information that you have. Then ask your partner for the information you are missing. Write it on the map. Use the worksheet.

Ask: What is the distance between Winnipeg and Ottawa?

Say: The distance between Winnipeg and Toronto is 2099 kilometres.

Map B

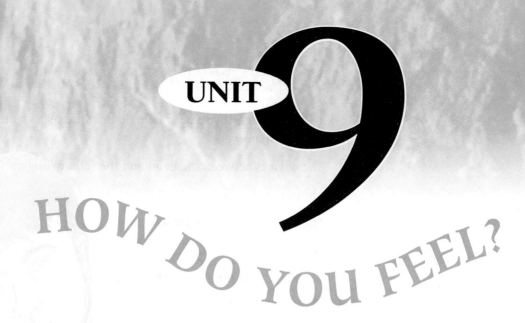

HOW DO YOU FEEL?

QUIZ: HEALTH

Before you start the unit, try this vocabulary quiz. Work with a partner. Choose the best answers.

1. If you sneeze and cough, you probably have:

   a) a cold

   b) a headache

   c) a cut

2. A thermometer is used to check:

   a) if you have a cough

   b) if you have a fever

   c) if you have an earache

3. To see a doctor in Canada you need:

   a) a social insurance card

   b) an identification card

   c) a health insurance card

4. For medical emergencies you should:

   a) go to a clinic

   b) make an appointment with the doctor

   c) call an ambulance

5. If you think you have a broken bone, you may need:

   a) a prescription

   b) an X-ray

   c) a bandaid

6. A stethoscope is used to check:

   a) the chest

   b) the ears

   c) the neck

OUR BODIES

 Work with a partner. If you need help, look at the picture on page 121. Choose the best answers.

1. The wrist is between the hand and the (elbow/fingers).

2. Above the eyes is the (chin/forehead).

3. The knee is on the (leg/arm).

4. Between the ankles and the hips are the (knees/wrists).

5. The toes are at the ends of the (hands/feet).

6. The cheeks are below the (eyes/knees).

7. Between the wrist and the shoulder is the (ankle/elbow).

8. A beard is on the (chin/forehead).

9. The waist is between the chest and the (hips/shoulders).

10. The eyebrows are on the (chin/forehead).

11. The chest is above the (waist/neck).

12. Between the chin and the shoulders is the (neck/back).

13. The fingers are at the ends of the (feet/hands).

14. On the eyes are the (eyelashes/moustache).

15. The hips are (above/below) the waist.

16. A moustache is on the (lip/chin).

17. The neck is below the (waist/chin).

18. The eyelashes are (above/below) the eyebrows.

19. The thumb is on the (hand/foot)

20. Inside the mouth is the (tongue/lips).

CANADIAN CAPSULES   Children and teenagers should not take aspirin without consulting a doctor. This is because aspirin is believed to be related to a rare disease called Reye's syndrome that can be very serious, especially for children.

HOW TO DRAW A HAPPY FACE

 Work in pairs. Follow the instructions to draw a happy face. Use a notebook. Have fun!

1.   Student A: Draw an oval for the face.

2.   Student B: Draw eyes on the face.

3.   Student A: Draw a nose in the middle of the face.

4.   Student B: Draw ears on the sides of the face.

5.   Student A: Draw a smiling mouth with some teeth.

6.   Student B: Draw eyelashes and eyebrows above the eyes.

7.   Student A: Draw hair on the head. Choose a hairstyle you like: long or short, curly or straight.

8.   Student B: Add these things if you want to: a beard, a moustache.

9.   Student A: Add these things if you want to: glasses, earrings, a necklace.

10.   Student B: Add anything you want to complete the drawing.

Together: Now you can name the person in your drawing and show it to other students. Does the person look like anyone you know?

GETTING SICK

 Work with a partner. Match the problem to the picture.

1.   a headache
2.   a backache
3.   a sore throat
4.   a sore shoulder
5.   a sore knee
6.   a stomachache
7.   a toothache

8.   to sneeze
9.   to cough
10. a fever
11. a cut
12. a broken bone
13. a sprain
14. a rash

I THINK I'M CATCHING A COLD

Use these words to complete the paragraph.

cold   bed   well   winter   tired   throat   snow   cough

It's __1_____. The weather is cold and damp. There is __2_____ on the ground. I don't feel __3_____. I think I'm catching a __4_____. Yesterday I sneezed all day. Today my __5_____ is sore. Tomorrow, I'll probably have a __6_____. I feel __7_____ and weak. I think I'd better go to __8_____.

TALK ABOUT IT

1. What are some symptoms of a cold?

2. How often do you get colds?

3. What do you do when you have a cold?

4. What are some things people can do to feel better when they have a cold?

5. Do you think it's a good idea to go to the doctor when you have a cold? Why or why not?

6. Look at the pictures. Which of these things do you use or take when you have a cold?

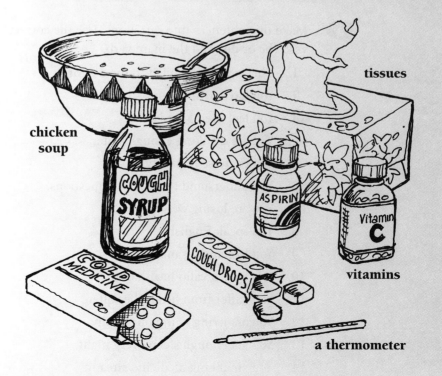

chicken soup

tissues

vitamins

a thermometer

AT THE DOCTOR

LISTENING ACTIVITY 15

A   Read the questions aloud with a partner.

B   Listen and answer the questions.

1. How does the patient feel?

2. What are the patient's symptoms?

3. What was wrong with the patient last week?

4. What symptom does the doctor ask about next?

5. What does the doctor use the stethoscope for?

6. What kind of test does the doctor mention?

7. What does the doctor say about antibiotics?

Turn to page 131 for Exercise C.

 GRAMMAR FOCUS

Question Words

To form questions, use the auxiliary verb before the subject of the sentence.

> We are going. **Are we going?**
>
> They go often. **Do they go often?**

A   Make the sentences into questions. Use the correct form of the auxiliary verb (**be** or **do**) and the main verb.

1. This is your first visit to the doctor.

2. You have pain in your stomach.

3. You feel tired a lot lately.

4. You are drinking enough water.

5. You exercise regularly.

6. You understand the doctor's questions.

7. You are losing weight.

8. You speak English.

9. You live at the same address.

10. You have a valid health card.

11. You suffer from headaches often.

12. You are living with your family.

13. You get enough sleep every night.

14. You are taking medicine already.

15. You take vitamins in the winter.

To ask for specific information, use WH-question words.

When	Time	**When** is the appointment?
Where	Location	**Where** is the office?
Who	People	**Who** did you talk to?
Why	Reason	**Why** are you late?
What	Things	**What** do you want?
How	Manner	**How** do you feel?
How old	Age	**How** old are you?
How much	Amounts	**How** much is it?

B Match the questions and the answers.

1. Who did you ask?   a) at 3 o'clock

2. How old is he?   b) my wallet

3. Why is it cold?   c) $15.39

4. When is the meeting?   d) by car

5. What did you lose?   e) downtown

6. How did they come?   f) 36

7. How much is it?   g) It's winter.

8. Where do you live?   h) the doctor

C Complete the conversations with WH-question words.

1. a) I can't find my car keys.

   b) _____ did you leave them?

2. a) We can't come to class tomorrow.

   b) Really? _____ not?

3. a) You should park in the parking lot.

   b) _____ does it cost?

4. a) I have pneumonia.

   b) _____ do you know?

5. a) We have a meeting at the office sometime soon.

   b) _____ is it going to take place?

6. a) I just had my birthday last week.

   b) _____ were you?

7. a) Nobody knows where the emergency room is.

   b) _____ did you ask?

8. a) Oh no. I think I forgot something.

   b) _____ did you forget?

9. a) That car is really expensive.

   b) _____ does it cost?

10. a) They didn't take the bus today.

    b) _____ did they get here?

IN THE MARTIN HOUSEHOLD

The last few months have been difficult at the Martin household. Everyone was sick or hurt, and the family had to call the doctor several times.

A Look at the pictures. What kind of problems did the family have?

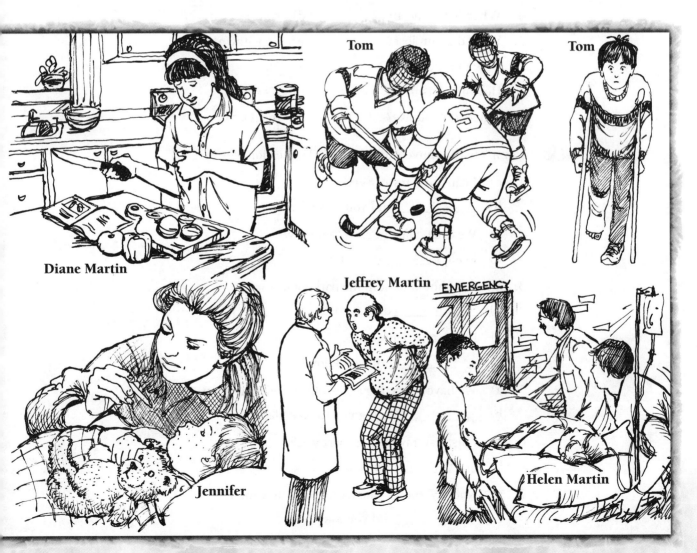

B Read about the Martin family.

In the Martin Household

On February 6, 36-year-old Diane Martin hurt her thumb while she was preparing supper. As she was cutting an onion, the knife slipped and she cut her thumb badly. She put a band-aid on the cut, but it was still bleeding. Finally she went to the emergency room at the hospital. A doctor examined the cut, and put in three stitches.

A few weeks later, on March 11, Tom, Diane's ten-year-old son, was playing hockey in the rink at the park. He and another hockey player bumped into each other. Tom fell down hard and hurt his ankle. He thought his ankle was broken, so his parents took him to the emergency room. A doctor examined Tom, and took an X-ray. She said that the ankle was broken. She put a cast on Tom's leg and gave him crutches. She said he would need the cast for about six weeks.

On April 17, Jennifer Martin, who is six years old, found spots on her arms and legs. Soon she had a rash all over her body. She had a fever and felt very sick. Diane took her to the doctor. The doctor said that Jennifer had chicken pox, a common childhood disease that would go away by itself in a week to ten days. The important thing was for Jennifer to try not to scratch her spots.

On May 4, Diane's husband, Jeffrey Martin, 40 years old, hurt his back. He didn't know how it happened, but when he woke up in the morning, his back was very sore. He went to the doctor to ask what to do. The doctor gave him some simple exercises and told him to rest for a few days.

About a week later, on May 12, Helen Martin, Jeffrey's 76-year-old mother, had bad pains in her chest. She called Diane and Jeffrey in the middle of the night. Her son and daughter-in-law thought she might be having a heart attack, so they called an ambulance to take her to the hospital. The doctors at the hospital examined her. They said they were not sure what was causing the pain, but they decided to keep her in the hospital for a few days to do more tests.

CANADIAN CAPSULES

If someone is not breathing, or is suffering severe chest pains, call an ambulance or take that person immediately to the emergency room of the nearest hospital.

C Copy the chart below, and write the information in the chart. Put an ✘ if you have no information.

Patient's name	Age	Problem	Date	Type of treatment	Length of treatment

TALK ABOUT IT

Talk about a medical problem that you or someone you know had.

1. What was the problem?

2. What were the symptoms?

3. Did you call a doctor or go to the emergency room?

4. What was the treatment?

5. How long did it take for the problem to go away?

6. Do you have any advice for someone with this problem?

ROLE PLAY: FEELING SICK

Work with a partner. One person is the doctor. The other is the patient. Write a dialogue about feeling sick. Act it out.

CANADIAN CAPSULES   To find a family doctor, ask friends who they recommend.

I WAS WONDERING . . .
HOW IS THIS CARD USED?

LISTENING ACTIVITY 16

 A   Read the questions aloud with a partner.

 B   Listen and answer the questions.

1. Who did Rosa come to Halifax with?

2. What will she do for the first time?

3. What does she ask Susan about?

4. Why is she going to the medical clinic?

5. What does Susan offer to do?

6. Why was Rosa going to go to the medical clinic alone?

7. What does Susan tell Rosa to do with the card at the clinic?

8. Where does the government get money to pay our medical bills?

9. What two things does Rosa thank Susan for?

10. Why does Susan suggest they hurry?

C   Match the expressions with the meanings.

1. It's actually…   a) to accompany someone

2. No problem.   b) to go quickly

3. to come with someone   c) It's OK.

4. It's my pleasure.   d) In fact, it's…

5. to hurry   e) I am happy to do it.

JOURNAL: A MEDICAL PROBLEM

Write about a medical problem you or someone you know had. What was the problem? How was it treated?

TEN-MINUTE GAMES AND ACTIVITIES

What's True?

1. Take a piece of paper. Write three sentences about your health or lifestyle. Write two sentences that are false. Write one sentence that is true.

> I exercise every day.
>
> I broke my arm playing hockey.
>
> I eat hamburgers for lunch almost every day.

2. Work in a group. Read your sentences to your group.

3. Everyone guesses which sentence is true by asking questions.

What Goes With What?

Each word in Box A has a match in Box B. Find the words that go together.

Box A

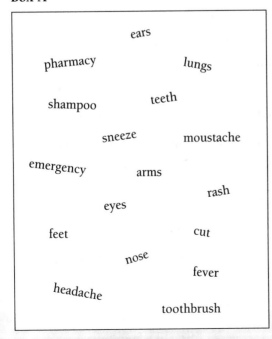

ears

pharmacy   lungs

shampoo   teeth

sneeze   moustache

emergency   arms

            rash

eyes

feet   cut

    nose

        fever

headache

    toothbrush

Box A

walk

see   smell

thermometer   hair

    tissues   medicine

beard   stitches

            carry

    chew

ointment   breathe

    aspirin   ambulance

hear   toothpaste

AT THE DOCTOR

LISTENING ACTIVITY 15

C Listen and complete the conversation. Use the worksheet.

Doctor: What _____ I do for you?

Patient: I don't feel well, doctor. I _____ really sick.

Doctor: What _____ your symptoms?

Patient: I have a bad cough, especially at night. And my chest hurts.

Doctor: Do you _____ a cold?

Patient: Yes, I was sneezing a lot last week, and I had a sore throat.

Doctor: _____ you have a fever?

Patient: No, I don't think _____.

Doctor: Well, I'll listen to your chest with the stethoscope. We may have to send _____ for an X-ray.

Patient: Do you think I need _____ take antibiotics?

Doctor: That depends _____ the X-ray. If it's just a bad cold, you don't need antibiotics. Just rest in bed. You should _____ better in a few days.

D Practise the conversation with a partner.

QUIZ: LEISURE ACTIVITIES

Before you start the unit, try this vocabulary quiz. Work with a partner. Choose the best answers.

1. Which activity is **not** a sport?

   a) hockey

   b) gardening

   c) tennis

2. Which sport does **not** use a net?

   a) basketball

   b) badminton

   c) swimming

3. Which sport **cannot** be played inside a building?

   a) skating

   b) hockey

   c) skiing

4. Which activity do you **not** do sitting down?

   a) sewing

   b) reading

   c) cooking

5. For which sport do you **not** need a bathing suit?

   a) aerobics

   b) swimming

   c) diving

6. Which activity does **not** need a partner?

   a) playing chess

   b) fishing

   c) judo

Discuss these questions in a group.

1. Do you play a sport? What is it?
2. Do you have a hobby? What is it?
3. Do you have a pet? What kind?
4. Do you watch movies? Which ones?
5. Do you like music? Which kind?

FUN AND GAMES

Look at the pictures of people doing things in their spare time. Find these sports and activities:

gardening	fishing	playing chess
aerobic exercise	ice skating	swimming
hockey	watching TV	painting
basketball	playing music	reading
knitting	dancing	collecting stamps
playing tennis	listening to music	cooking
playing soccer	jogging	camping
walking a dog	in-line skating	sewing
judo		

THE SPARE TIME QUIZ

A   Read the paragraph. Then close your book. Write as your teacher dictates.

People do many different things in their spare time. This is the time they use to do things they really enjoy. They play sports, work on a hobby, take care of a pet, or choose some kind of entertainment such as television, movies, music, or shows. What do you like to do in your spare time?

B   Work in groups of four to do this quiz. Read the questions and discuss the answers. Choose the best answers.

1. The most popular sport in Canada is:

   a) soccer

   b) hockey

   c) baseball

2. William Shakespeare was a great:

   a) writer

   b) singer

   c) swimmer

3. The first animal to become a pet was the:

   a) dog

   b) cat

   c) bird

4. Which sport is not played in the Olympic Games?

   a) judo

   b) ice hockey

   c) fishing

5. The number of hours of television the average child in North America watches each week is:

   a) 15

   b) 22

   c) 31

6. The most popular sport in the world is:

   a) swimming

   b) baseball

   c) soccer

7. Tennis began in:

   a) Germany

   b) England

   c) France

8. The most popular musical band of all time was:

   a) The Rolling Stones

   b) The Beatles

   c) Guns 'n' Roses

9. Judo comes from:

   a) Japan

   b) Korea

   c) Vietnam

10. Ballet is a kind of:

    a) sport

    b) dance

    c) music

11. Baseball is the most popular sport in:

    a) the United States

    b) Mexico

    c) Argentina

12. A "musical" is a kind of:

    a) play

    b) song

    c) instrument

C When you have finished, turn to page 145. Read the text to check your answers.

CANADIAN CAPSULES

Canada has many outdoor areas where people can explore nature. In winter, people ski and snowshoe. In summer, they swim and fish in lakes and rivers. People also like to hike in the woods or ride bicycles on country roads.

DO YOU WANT TO GO SKATING?

LISTENING ACTIVITY 17

 A Look at the picture. Answer the questions with a partner.

1. What are the people doing?

2. What kind of clothes are they wearing?

3. What kind of equipment do they need?

 B Read the questions aloud with a partner.

C Listen and answer the questions.

1. When does Karen want to go skating?

2. Which two places does Mike ask about?

3. What can happen to the ice if the temperature goes up?

4. What is the time for free skating at the arena?

5. What is the arena used for the rest of the time?

6. Why does Mike want to go early?

7. What does Karen suggest they do after skating?

Turn to page 146 for Exercise D.

 **"Be going to" for Future Plans**

Use **be going to** for future plans. Put the auxiliary verb phrase **be going to** before the base form of the main verb.

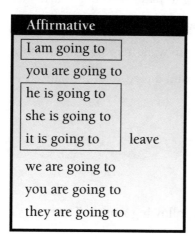
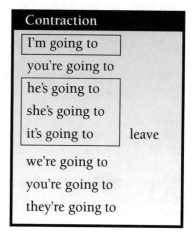

Affirmative	
I am going to	
you are going to	
he is going to	
she is going to	
it is going to	leave
we are going to	
you are going to	
they are going to	

Contraction	
I'm going to	
you're going to	
he's going to	
she's going to	
it's going to	leave
we're going to	
you're going to	
they're going to	

 A Change these sentences to the future. Use **be going to**.

1. Kim eats supper at six o'clock.

2. Max plays chess on Thursdays.

3. Nadia takes pictures on holidays.

4. Lili studies the guitar.

5. Geoff walks his dog after school.

6. Carlos and Ana watch the news at eight o'clock.

7. Paul and Mike play football on Sundays.

8. Gina collects stamps for her album.

9. My cousins swim in the ocean.

10. We go to the movies on Tuesdays.

11. Our friends meet us at the pool.

12. Tim and Tina skate on the weekend.

13. Everyone goes dancing on Saturdays.

14. Barbara cooks when she is home.

15. Jun watches TV if he has no homework.

B   Some sentences have errors. Find the errors and correct them.

1. She is going play tennis tomorrow.

2. I am going to watch a movie tonight.

3. We going to plant flowers in the garden this summer.

4. They are going eat in a Chinese restaurant on Friday.

5. Julie and Tom is going to dance at the disco tonight.

6. Bob is going to skate in the outdoor rink.

7. Marie are going to play chess in a tournament.

8. Ray and Victor are going do judo.

9. Laurie is going to walk her dog early tomorrow morning.

10. Jean is going paint a picture of the sunset.

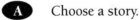

FAVOURITE PASTIMES

A   Choose a story.

1. Read one of the following stories. The first is about pets. The second is about hockey.

2. Find a partner who has chosen the same reading.

3. Read the story and answer the questions together.

4. Practise telling your story with your partner.

5. Write five discussion question about your story.

B   Exchange information.

1. Work with new partners. A student who has read "Why We Have Pets" works with a partner who has read "Hockey."

2. Tell your story to your partner.

3. Discuss the questions you wrote.

Why We Have Pets

For thousands of years, in every part of the world, people have kept animals as pets. Over half the families in North America today own a pet. The most popular pets are dogs, cats, fish, and birds, but rabbits, hamsters, and turtles are also popular. Some people keep unusual animals, such as frogs, monkeys, and snakes. In Japan, mice are popular pets. Children tame the mice and teach them to dance to music.

People first started to keep pets about 12 000 years ago. The first animal to be kept as a pet was the dog. The dog became a pet because it was useful. It warned people of danger and it ate leftover food that could attract wild animals. Cats became pets when they were tamed by the Egyptians. When the Egyptians started to grow grain, mice ate it, so cats were needed to protect the grain.

Today, people keep many kinds of pets. All of these pets need care. Small animals such as birds and hamsters need people to bring them food and water and keep their cages clean. Dogs need to be walked every day, although a small dog can get most of its exercise by playing around the house. Cats are quieter and more independent than dogs, but they still need to be fed and petted.

Some people choose pets that are useful. For example, dogs can protect people's homes and can help people who are blind or deaf or who can't use their arms or legs. But most people have pets for pleasure. Pets can be good friends for people, especially for children and seniors.

Questions

1. Name some popular pets.

2. Name some unusual pets.

3. What kind of pet is popular with children in Japan?

4. When did people first start to keep pets?

5. Explain how dogs were useful to people.

6. Why did the Egyptians keep cats as pets?

7. How do people take care of animals in cages?

8. What kind of care do dogs need?

9. How are cats different from dogs?

10. How can dogs help people?

11. What is the main reason people have pets?

Hockey

Hockey is a fast, exciting sport that began in Canada in the 1800s. Every year thousands of Canadians play hockey or watch the game on television.

Hockey is played on a sheet of ice called a rink. Two teams compete to score points by shooting a puck into a net. Each team has six players who skate on the ice. Hockey is one of the fastest sports. When players shoot the puck, it can travel more than 160 kilometres per hours. Goalkeepers try to keep the puck out of their nets.

Because hockey is a fast, rough game, the players need special clothing and equipment for protection. They wear helmets to protect their heads, as well as heavy sweaters, pants, and gloves. Children who play on teams usually wear the same clothing and equipment as professional players.

Hockey is a popular winter sport for children. In the city, children often play hockey in skating rinks in the park. In the country, children can play hockey on frozen ponds, lakes, or rivers. Many children play in teams, and compete with other teams. They spend long hours in the arena practising for their games.

In the past, all hockey games were played outside on frozen rivers and lakes. In the spring, there were sometimes accidents when players fell through the ice. Today, most hockey games take place in indoor arenas, so they don't have to stop when the weather gets warm.

Questions

1. When and where did hockey begin?
2. Where is hockey played?
3. How do teams score points?
4. How many players are on each team?
5. How fast can a puck move?
6. What do goalkeepers do?
7. What do hockey players wear to protect their heads?
8. What kind of clothing do hockey players wear?
9. Where do children play hockey in the following places?
    a) in cities
    b) in the country
    c) on teams
10. What happened in the spring in the past?
11. Why can hockey games take place even in warm weather today?

WHAT I LIKE TO DO

Chose a sport, hobby, or interest. Prepare a short talk for a group of students. Talk about these things:

1. What is your sport, hobby, or interest?

2. Where do you play or do it?

3. How you play or do it?

4. Why do you like it?

JOURNAL: IN MY SPARE TIME

Write about something you like to do in your spare time.

TEN-MINUTE GAMES AND ACTIVITIES

What Doesn't Belong?

In each group, **one or two** words don't belong. Work with a partner to find the words that don't belong.

1. Sports that use a ball:
   a) tennis
   b) hockey
   c) soccer
   d) basketball

2. Things you listen to:
   a) a radio
   b) classical music
   c) a violin
   d) judo

3. Things you read:
   a) books
   b) paintings
   c) newspapers
   d) magazines

4. Activities you play:
   a) chess
   b) checkers
   c) piano
   d) skating

5. Activities you can do indoors:
   a) swim
   b) ski
   c) walk your dog
   d) cook

6. Activities you do with your hands:
   a) cook
   b) knit
   c) sew
   d) play soccer

7. Activities you do alone:
    a) read
    b) play tennis
    c) cook
    d) swim

8. Activities you do sitting down:
    a) dance
    b) go fishing
    c) watch movies
    d) collect stamps

9. Activities you can do in a team:
    a) sew
    b) paint
    c) play hockey
    d) swim

10. Pets that can stay indoors all the time:
    a) cats
    b) birds
    c) turtles
    d) dogs

Activity Ratings

Work in a group to rate the activities below. Use the listed categories. Rate each activity for each category. For example, which activity is the most interesting? Which activity is the least interesting? Put the activities in order from most to least. Then continue with the next category.

Try to reach a consensus in your group. Then compare your list with the results of other groups in the class.

Categories	**Activities**
interesting	1. walking a dog
fun	2. playing hockey
dangerous	3. going fishing
difficult	4. cooking
	5. collecting stamps
	6. playing piano

CANADIAN CAPSULES   Canada has seven teams in the National Hockey League (NHL).

1. Hockey began in Canada about 100 years ago. It soon became a major Canadian sport. Today it is Canada's most popular form of entertainment. Everyone likes to talk about the latest hockey game.

2. Perhaps the greatest English writer of all time was William Shakespeare. He wrote many plays, which are still performed all over the world today. Shakespeare lived in England. He died in 1616.

3. People first started to keep pets about 12 000 years ago. The first pet was a dog. It became a pet because it was useful in keeping wild animals away. Cats became pets soon after, and were useful in catching mice.

4. The Olympic Games are held every four years, in different countries of the world. They are the most important competition for amateur athletes. Ice hockey is a winter sport that is played in the Olympics. Judo is a summer sport. Fishing is not an Olympic sport.

5. In North America there are about 365 television sets for every 1000 people. The average child between the ages of 2 and 11 watches about 31 hours of TV per week.

6. Soccer is the most popular sport in the world. In some countries it is called football. More than one billion people play soccer in over 150 countries.

7. Tennis began in England in 1873. The first championship matches were held at Wimbledon, near London. Today people play tennis all over the world.

8. The most popular band of all time was the Beatles, who were as famous for their hair and clothes as they were for their music. A whole generation knows the songs of the Beatles. Many of these songs have become classics today.

9. Judo comes from Japan. It means "gentle way." It is a popular sport all over the world. People learn judo to exercise, relax, and protect themselves.

10. There are many different kinds of dance. Dance can be used to show feeling or ideas, or it can be done just for fun. Ballet is a form of dance that began in Europe in the 1600s. Now it is mostly done by women, but in the beginning all the ballet dancers were men!

11. Baseball is so popular in the United States that it is called the national pastime. Millions of people watch baseball on television, and play baseball too. Most of the games take place in spring and summer.

12. A musical is a kind of play that has lively music and songs, dances, and colourful costumes. It often tells a story and uses the songs and dance to express the characters' feelings.

DO YOU WANT TO GO SKATING?

LISTENING ACTIVITY 17

D Listen and write the words. Use the worksheet.

Karen: Do you want _____ go skating on Saturday, Mike?

Mike: _____ Karen. Where do you want to go—the rink in _____ park, or the arena?

Karen: Well, it depends _____ the weather. It's cold today, but I heard the temperature is supposed to go _____. If that happens, the ice might melt a bit and it will be too soft to skate outside.

Mike: Yeah, _____ right. Let's go to the arena then. Do you know what time it's open?

Karen: Yes, there's free skating between two and four o'clock. The rest of the time the _____ is reserved for hockey practice.

Mike: OK, but let's go a little early. I _____ to sharpen the blades on my skates.

Karen: No problem. Maybe we can go _____ hot chocolate after.

Mike: _____ a great idea.

E Practise the conversation with a partner.

Community Contact Task 1

Set up a time to meet with a partner to explore something in one of your neighbourhoods—for example, a restaurant, a recreation centre, a sports arena, a store, a theatre, etc.

Choose a place you have never been before.

Report your experience to the class. Did you like the place you explored? Why or why not?

Community Contact Task 2

Go to a store in your neighbourhood that sells bread. Find four different kinds of bread or rolls. Then answer the questions.

1. Where did you go?

    a) a bakery   c) a grocery store

    b) a supermarket   d) other

2. What was the name of the store?

3. What were the names of the breads you found?

    a) white sliced   g) French bread

    b) rye bread   h) bagel

    c) corn bread   i) rolls

    d) pumpernickel   j) pita

    e) whole wheat   k) other

    f) oatmeal

4. How much did the bread or package cost?

    a) less than $1.00   c) more than $1.50

    b) more than $1.00   d) more than $2.00

5. The bread was:

    a) on a shelf   d) in a box

    b) on a counter   e) in a basket

    c) in a bag   f) other

Community Contact Task 3

Bring in a kind of food that your family eats at home. Eat lunch together. Share your food.

First make a chart to plan what each student in the class will bring.

Name of student	Main course	Dessert	Drink	Other
Maria	Lasagna			
Ali			Cola	

Write the name of the food and the main ingredients on a card. Put the card beside the food. Everyone gets to taste different kinds of food.

Community Contact Task 4

We need exact change to do these things:

- Use a public phone
- Take a city bus
- Buy a newspaper on the street
- Use a vending machine
- Park at a parking meter
- Use a washing machine
- Buy stamps at a stamp machine

Find the information to complete this chart.

	Total cost	Change needed
Public phone	.25	1 x 25¢
		2 x 10¢ + 1 x 5¢
Bus		
Newspaper		
Vending machine		
Parking meter		
Washing machine		
Stamp machine		

150

Community Contact Task 5

Go to a department store. On the chart, fill in three things you can buy in each department. Give the prices.

	Things you find	Price
Household furnishings	e.g., a lamp	$20.00
Shoes	e.g., slippers	
Clothes	e.g., a sweater	
Sports equipment	e.g., a tennis racket	

Community Contact Task 6

Imagine that you need to buy a new coat or jacket. Go to a clothing store or the clothing department of a department store. Choose a coat or jacket. (Don't buy it.)

Describe the coat or jacket you chose. Be sure to give the following information:

- Type (winter coat, spring coat, jacket, raincoat)
- Colour
- Size
- Price
- Number of buttons
- Number of pockets
- Does it have:
  - a lining?
  - a hood?
  - a zipper?
  - a belt?

Community Contact Task 7

In Class

Work in a group. Choose a city or town that you would like to visit.

In the Community

1. Find out the telephone number for Via Rial.

2. Call Via Rail. Get information about the schedule for trains to the city you have chosen. Use the touch-tone services if you have a touch-tone phone.

3. Find out:

    a) the times of departure on a week-day morning

    b) the times of return on Sunday evening

    c) the cost of a round-trip ticket

Note: With a touch-tone phone, you can call as many times as you like to listen to the information.

Reporting Back

In your group, compare your information.

Community Contact Task 8

In Class

Work with a partner. Choose a place in Canada you would like to visit on a weekend trip. Make a list of questions you will ask a travel agent. You will need information about transportation, places to stay, etc.

In the Community

With your partner, go to a travel agent. Ask the questions on your list. Write down the answers. You can also ask for brochures about the place you want to visit.

Reporting Back

In a group, compare your information.

Appendix 1: Spelling

Spelling Verb Forms Ending "ing"

The spelling rules for continuous verbs are different from the rules for regular past tense verbs. For example, with the verb **try**, the past tense is **tried**, but the continuous tense is **trying**.

Rule 1   Verbs that end with **e** drop the **e** and add **ing**:

write   writing

Rule 2   Verbs that end with two consonants (**n**, **d**, **k**, **b**, etc.) or with two vowels (a, e, i, o, u) add **ing**:

try   trying
read   reading

Rule 3   Verbs that end with a vowel and a consonant double the final letter and add **ing**:

put   putting

Exceptions: consonants **w**, **x**, and **y**. (**buy**   **buying**)

Note: Verbs that end **ie** change the **i** to **y** and add **ing**:

die   dying
lie   lying

Spelling Simple Past Tense

2 consonants	add **ed**	work	work**ed**
2 vowels + consonant	add **ed**	need	need**ed**
vowel + **y**	add **ed**	play	play**ed**
consonant + **y**	change **y** to **i** add **ed**	try	tri**ed**
vowel + consonant	double consonant add **ed**	plan	plann**ed**

Not all verbs that end in vowel + consonant double the final letter. Common exceptions are **listened**, **opened**, **answered**.

Spelling Rules with Comparative Forms

Adjectives that end in **y** change **y** to **i** and add **er** for the comparative or **est** for the superlative form:

happy   happier
silly   silliest

Adjectives that end in vowel + consonant double the final letter and add **er** for the comparative or **est** for the superlative form:

fat	fatter
thin	thinner

Spelling Plural Nouns

Nouns that end in **s**, **ch**, **sh**, **z**, **o** add **es** to form the plural:

watch	watches
box	boxes
potato	potatoes

Nouns that end in consonant + **y** change the **y** to **i** and add **es** for the plural form:

city	cities
activity	activities

Nouns that end in vowel + **y** add **s**:

day	days
key	keys

Nouns that end in **f** or **fe** change the **f** to **v** and add **es** to form the plural:

leaf	leaves
knife	knives

Irregular Plurals

person	people
child	children
woman	women
man	men
mouse	mice
foot	feet
tooth	teeth
ox	oxen

Appendix 2: Irregular Past Tense Verbs

Present	Past
arise	arose
awake	awoke
be	was, were
beat	beat
become	became
begin	began
bite	bit
bleed	bled
blow	blew
break	broke
bring	brought
build	built
buy	bought
catch	caught
choose	chose
come	came
cost	cost
cut	cut
dig	dug
do	did
draw	drew
drink	drank
drive	drove
eat	ate
fall	fell
feed	fed
feel	felt
find	found
fly	flew
forbid	forbade
forget	forgot

Present	Past
forgive	forgave
freeze	froze
get	got
give	gave
go	went
grow	grew
have	had
hear	heard
hide	hid
hit	hit
hold	held
hurt	hurt
keep	kept
know	knew
lay	laid
lead	led
leave	left
let	let
lie	lay
lose	lost
make	made
mean	meant
meet	met
pay	paid
put	put
read	read
ride	rode
ring	rang
rise	rose
run	ran
see	saw

Present	Past
sell	sold
send	sent
shake	shook
shine	shone
shoot	shot
show	showed
shrink	shrank
shut	shut
sing	sang
sit	sat
sleep	slept
speak	spoke
spread	spread
spring	sprang
stand	stood
steal	stole
stink	stank
swear	swore
swim	swam
take	took
teach	taught
tear	tore
tell	told
think	thought
throw	threw
understand	understood
wake	woke
wear	wore
win	won
write	wrote

Englisch ist einfach

ben englizce oranmak stiurum

私は英語が好きです。

أنا أحب هذا الكتاب

Vaya suka buku ini

Bu kitapi cok seudim

我會說英文

See you in Canadian Concepts 4!

Delam mikhad englisi yad begiram

နွေနှာ နွေနှာ   Mi piace molto questo
libro

Tôi thích quyển sách này

Inglês é fácil de aprender.

Je parle l'anglais

안녕

Μιλαω Εγγλινικά

ME GUSTA HABLAR INGLES

Μου αρέσει αυτό το βιβλίο

私はこの本が大好きです。